Selections from the

World's Devotional Classics

Volume V

Scupoli to Whichcote

Laurence (Lorenzo) Scupoli

Selections
from the
World's Devotional Classics

EDITED BY

Robert Scott and George W. Gilmore

Editors of The Homiletic Review

———

IN TEN VOLUMES

———

Volume V
Scupoli to Whichcote

FUNK & WAGNALLS COMPANY

NEW YORK AND LONDON

242
S428s
v.5

Contents Volume Five

Selections

Prayers

SELECTIONS FROM

The Spiritual Combat

AND

The Path of Paradise

BY

LAURENCE SCUPOLI

FROM THE TRANSLATION

BY

THE REV. W. H. HUTCHINGS, M.A.

LAURENCE (LORENZO) SCUPOLI

An ascetical writer of the Theatine Order, born at Otranto in 1530; died at Naples November 28, 1610. He entered the Theatine monastery of St. Paul at Naples in 1570; showed great talent as preacher and was sent out by his order to preach in Placentia, Milan, Genoa, Venice, and Naples. His fame cost him slander and jealousy. He retired to his cell, the principal fruit of this retirement being "The Spiritual Combat" (Venice, 1589; fifty editions were printed before his death; translations were made into all the principal European languages and into Latin and Armenian). He wrote also "The Peace of the Soul" and other pastoral and devotional tracts.

The Spiritual Combat

In What Christian Perfection Consists; and That the Attainment of It Involves a Struggle, and of Four Things Necessary for This Conflict

If you wish, beloved in Christ, to reach the height of perfection, and by drawing near to God to become one spirit with him (and no enterprise can be imagined or exprest which is greater, or nobler than this), you must before all else gain a true idea of what constitutes genuine spiritual perfection.

There are many who have believed it to consist exclusively in outward mortification, in hair-shirts and disciplines, in long watchings and fastings, and in other bodily sufferings and chastisements.

Others again, and especially women, think that they have reached the climax of perfection, when they say many prayers, attend many services and offices, and are regularly at church and at communion.

Some indeed (and amongst this class not a few religious persons who have withdrawn themselves from the world), persuade themselves that perfection entirely depends on the

By kind permission of Longmans, Green & Co., New York.

regular attendance at the hours of prayer, on silence, solitude, and exact observance of rule.

And thus, some in these, and others in other similar actions suppose perfection to consist. But they are all deceived. For altho these practises are sometimes means of gaining the spirit of perfection, and sometimes are its fruits, yet in no sense can it ever be said that true spiritual perfection consists in these alone.

Unquestionably they are means most efficacious for obtaining spirituality, when they are properly and discreetly employed; for by them we gain strength against our own sinfulness and frailty, we are fortified against the assaults and snares of our common enemies, and, in short, are provided with those spiritual helps which are necessary to all the servants of God, and especially to those who have but lately entered upon his service.

They are likewise fruits of the Spirit in truly spiritual persons, who "keep under" the body because it has offended its Maker, and for the sake of humbling it and making it subject to his commands; in those who live in solitude and silence in order to avoid even the least occasions of sin, and to have their conversation in heaven, and who give themselves entirely to the service of God and to works of mercy; who pray, and meditate upon the life and passion of Jesus Christ, not for the sake of curiosity and devotional feeling, but that they may gain deeper knowledge of their own corruptness and of God's mercy and goodness, and that they may be more and more inflamed with the love of God, and the hatred of themselves—following the Son of God by self-denial, and by taking the cross upon their shoulders; who receive the blessed sacrament with the view of glorifying the divine Majesty, of being more closely united with God, and of gaining fresh strength against their enemies.

To others, however, who found perfection entirely on external practises, such works may bring greater ruin than open sins; not that these works are bad in themselves, for in themselves they are very good, but in consequence of the mistaken use which is made of them they have this sad result; because those who practise them are so wrapt up in what they do, that they leave their hearts a prey to their own evil inclinations and to the wiles of Satan. He sees them wandering from the right path, and not only does he leave them to the enjoyment of these exercises, but lets them vainly fancy that they are roaming amidst the delights of paradise, and persuade themselves that they are borne upward even to the angelic choirs, and that they feel the

5

presence of God within them. Such persons sometimes are so absorbed in curious, deep, delightful thoughts, that they become, as it were, oblivious of the world and of all creatures, and appear to themselves rapt even to the third heaven.

But in how great an error these persons have entangled themselves, and how far they are distant from that true perfection which we seek, may easily be gathered from their lives and habits. For in every thing, whether it be great or small, they seek their own advantage, and like to be preferred before others; they are self-willed and opinionated, blind to their own faults, sharp-sighted for the faults of others, and severely condemn the sayings and doings of other men.

But if you touch only with your finger a certain vain reputation in which they hold themselves, and are pleased to be held by others; if you bid them discontinue any of their regular and formal devotions, they are at once angry and exceedingly disturbed.

And if God himself visits them with trials and infirmities (which never come without his appointment or permission, and which are the tests of his servants' faithfulness), or if he permits them to be sorely persecuted in order that they may gain a true knowledge of themselves, and be brought back to the way of true perfection, immediately the false foundation is discovered, and the miserable condition of the proud heart is seen. For in all events, whether adverse or prosperous, they are unwilling to be resigned and to humble themselves under the mighty hand of God, acquiescing in his just tho hidden judgments; neither will they, in imitation of the most lowly and patient Son of God, abase themselves below all creatures, and love their persecutors and enemies as dear friends, because they are the instruments of divine Goodness, and work together for their mortification, perfection and salvation.

It is therefore quite evident, that all such persons are in great danger. For since the inward eye is darkened, by which they see themselves and their outward actions which are good, they attribute to themselves a high degree of perfection, and so, becoming more and more puffed up, they readily pass judgment upon others; yet they themselves need a special miracle of grace to convert them, for nothing short of that would have effect. It is more easy to convert and bring back an open sinner to the path of truth, than the man whose state is hidden and mantled with the semblance of virtue.

You clearly and distinctly see, then, from what I have said, that the essence of the spiritual life does not lie in any of those things to which I have alluded. It consists in nothing else but the knowledge of the divine Goodness and Greatness, of our own nothingness, and proneness to all evil; in the love of God and the hatred of self; in entire subjection not only to God himself, but, for the love of him, to all creatures; in giving up our own will, and in completely resigning ourselves to the divine pleasure; moreover, in willing and doing all this with no other wish or aim than the glory and honor of God, the fulfilment of his will because it is his will, and because he deserves to be served and loved.

This is the law of love, engraven on the hearts of his faithful servants by the hand of the Lord himself. This is the self-denial which is required of us. This is his sweet yoke and light burden. This is that obedience to which our Redeemer and Master calls us, both by word and example.

But if you aspire to such a pitch of perfection, you must daily do violence to yourself, by courageously attacking and destroying all your evil desires, in great matters as well as in small; it is necessary, then, that you prepare yourself and hold yourself in readiness for this conflict, for he only will be crowned who was brave in the battle.

Doubtless this is the hardest of all struggles, because by fighting against ourselves, we are, at the same time, attacked by ourselves, and on that account the victory obtained in such a conflict will be of all others the most glorious, and most dear to God.

Therefore, if you used every endeavor to mortify yourself, and to tread down your inordinate affections, inclinations, and rebellious passions, even in the smallest matters, you would be rendering to God a far greater and more acceptable service than if, whilst permitting some of your inclinations to remain unmortified, you scourged yourself until you bled, fasted more rigorously and practised an austerity greater than that of the hermits and saints of the desert, or converted souls by thousands.

For, altho in itself the conversion of souls is dearer to God than the mortification of an irregular desire, yet it is not your duty to will and perform that which is in itself more excellent, but that which God before all else strictly wills and requires of you. For he doubtless seeks and desires of you self-conquest, and the thorough mortification of your passions, rather than that you, wilfully leaving one of them alive in you, should perform in some other direction some greater and more notable service for his sake.

Now you see wherein the real perfection of a Christian lies, and that to obtain it you must enter upon a constant and sharp warfare against self; you must provide yourself with four very safe and highly necessary weapons, that you may win the palm, and be finally a conqueror in this spiritual conflict—these are:

Distrust of self; trust in God; spiritual exercises; prayer.

[Succeeding chapters deal with Distrust of Self, Trust in God, and Means of Obtaining These, and Spiritual Exercises as Applied to the Understanding.]

Of the Exercise of the Will, and of the End to Which All Our Actions, Both Inward and Outward, Should be Directed

In addition to this exercise which relates to the understanding, you must also discipline your will, so that it may not be left to follow its own desires, but be in all things conformed to the good pleasure of God.

And remember, that it is not enough that you should will and do those things which are most pleasing to God; but, beyond this, you must will and do them, as moved by him, and with the motive of simply pleasing him.

In this, even more than in the matter we

have been considering in the previous chapter, lies the struggle with our nature, which seeks itself and its own pleasures in all things; and most of all in good and spiritual things; in these nature delights itself, revelling in them, as it suspects no harm from such food.

As soon then as they are presented to us, we gaze longingly upon them and crave for them; not because we are moved to do the will of God and wish only to please him, but from a desire for that satisfaction and rest which we experience when we will those things which God wills.

The more excellent the object is which we desire, the more liable we are to be deceived. Thus, even in the desire after God himself, we are in danger of falling into the snares of self-love, by having an eye to our own interests and to the advantages which we expect from God, rather than to his will, whose pleasure it is that we should love, desire, and obey him simply for the sake of his glory.

I will now tell you how to avoid this delusion, which would hinder your progress in holiness; and how to get into the habit of willing and doing all things according to the guidance of the Spirit of God, and with the pure motive of honoring and serving him alone, who should be the beginning and end of all our thoughts and actions. When any thing presents itself as in accordance with the will of God, do not bring yourself to will it, until you have first lifted up your thoughts to God to ascertain whether it is his will that you should will it, and whether you will it because he does, and with the view of pleasing him alone. Then let your will—thus moved and drawn by his—be bent upon willing it, because he wills it, and with the sole object of pleasing and glorifying him.

The same course must be pursued in refusing the things which are contrary to God's will. Do not refuse them till you have first fixt the eye of the understanding upon his divine will, who wills that you should refuse them for the sake of pleasing him.

Know, however, that we little suspect how deceitful and crafty our nature is, which is ever secretly seeking self; for we are often led to imagine that our object and motive is to please God, when it is quite the reverse. Thus it comes to pass, that when we choose or refuse any thing for our own interest, we fancy that we are choosing or refusing it in the hope of pleasing, or fear of displeasing God.

The true and inward remedy for this delusion is purity of heart, which consists in this (which is really the aim of all this spiritual combat), namely—the putting off the old man, and the putting on the new.

In order to be well prepared, seeing you are full of self, beware at the beginning of every action, of any admixture of selfish motives, and free yourself as much as possible from them. Neither choose, nor do, nor refuse any thing, unless you feel yourself moved and drawn to that course by the pure and simple will of God.

If you can not always feel that you are actuated by this motive in your conduct, especially in the inward acts of the mind, or in short outward actions, you must rest satisfied that you virtually have it, from the habit of maintaining a pure intention of pleasing God alone in all you do.

But in actions which occupy some space of time, it is well not to be content with kindling this motive in your heart at the commencement of the action, but also to be careful to renew it frequently whilst the action is going on, and thus to preserve it alive to the very end. If you neglect to do this, you will be in danger of falling into a snare, which our natural self-love prepares (for it is always more inclined and ready to follow its own course than to yield to God), namely, that of changing unconsciously after a time the objects and aims which you had in view when you began the action.

The servant of God, unless he is alive to this

danger, often commences a work with the sole object of pleasing his Lord; but by degrees, and almost imperceptibly, he begins to take such pleasure in the work itself that, losing sight of the divine will, he turns aside and becomes attached to the satisfaction he experiences in doing it, and to the advantage or credit he gains from it.

Then, if God himself place some hindrance in his way, and the work is impeded by sickness, accident, or some one's interference, presently he is troubled and vexed, and begins to murmur at this or at that, not to say, sometimes even against God himself—too clear a proof that he was not wholly seeking the will of God, and that his motive was rotten and corrupt at its core.

For every soul which moves as God moves it, and aims at pleasing him only, does not wish for this more than for that; nor to have any thing unless God wills to give it, nor to have it except in the way and for the time he appoints: such a soul is equally contented, whether having or not having it. For in either case it obtains its purpose, and its wish is fulfilled, which was nothing else but the good pleasure of God.

Therefore keep yourself habitually recollected, and be diligent in directing all your actions to this perfect end.

And if sometimes you are moved to do good (according to the bent of your natural disposition) by fear of the pains of hell or hope of the joys of heaven, you may even through these motives look ultimately to the good pleasure and will of God, who delights not at your departure into hell, but at your entrance into his kingdom.

The dignity and power of this motive no man can fully comprehend; a single action—even the least and most insignificant—done with the view of pleasing God alone and of glorifying him, is worth infinitely more (so to speak) than many actions in themselves of the greatest value and worth, but springing from other motives. Thus, a single penny given to a poor man, with the sole object of pleasing his divine majesty, is more acceptable in his sight than the entire renunciation of all our possessions, however great they may be, from some other motive, even for the attainment of the bliss of heaven, which is an object not merely good, but one in the highest degree desirable.

This practise of doing every thing with the simple intention of pleasing God alone, appears difficult at first, but becomes easy and delightful by use, if we frequently fix our desires on God himself, and long after him with the warm affections of our hearts, as our only and highest Good—the One who deserves that all beings should seek him for himself, and should serve and love him above all things.

The more seriously and constantly we meditate upon the infinite excellence of God, the more fervent and frequent will these acts of the will become; and we shall easily acquire in this way the habit of performing every action out of love to that Lord, who alone is worthy of it.

Lastly, in order to gain this divine intention, I advise you to seek it from God by earnest prayer; and to meditate often upon the numberless blessings which God, out of pure love, and with no benefit to himself, has bestowed, and is still bestowing upon us.

Of Some Considerations Which May Induce the Will to Seek In All Things the Good Pleasure of God

Moreover, to render the will more inclined to desire in all things the good pleasure and the glory of God, call oftentimes to mind how in many ways he has first honored and loved you.

By creation—making you out of nothing, after his likeness; and by making all other creatures for your use.

By redemption—sending, not an angel, but his only-begotten Son, to redeem you, not with the corruptible price of silver and gold, but with his own precious blood and his most painful and ignominious death.

Consider, too, that every hour and every moment, he defends you from your enemies, fights for you by his grace, offers you continually in the sacrament of the altar his dear Son to be your spiritual strength and nourishment; is not this a token of the inestimable love and regard which the infinite God has for you? We can not, on the one hand, conceive how much value so great a Lord sets on us poor creatures, in our baseness and misery; and, on the other, how much we are indebted to his high Majesty, who has done so many and so great things for us.

For if earthly masters, when they are honored even by men of poor and lowly condition, feel bound to honor them in return, how should our vileness behave itself toward the Sovereign Ruler of the universe, by whom we are so dearly prized and loved!

And, in addition to what has been already mentioned, keep ever in lively remembrance, that the divine Majesty is infinitely worthy to be honored and served simply for himself and for his own good pleasure.

Of the Many Wills Which Are In Man, and of the Warfare Between Them

Altho in this spiritual combat man has two wills—the will of the mind, which we call the reasonable and superior will; and the will of the senses, which we call the sensual and inferior will, and which sometimes bears the names of "appetite," "flesh," "sense," and "passion": yet, as it is through the reason that we are men, we can not be said to will any thing when the lower will desires it, unless the higher will is disposed also to consent to it.

And herein lies the whole spiritual struggle; the reasonable will stands midway between the divine will which is above it, and the lower will of the flesh which is below it, and is continually assailed by the one or the other; each seeking to attract it, to bring it into subjection, and to rule it.

Great is the toil and struggle at the outset, which beginners experience when they resolve to amend their wicked lives, and—renouncing the world and the flesh—to yield themselves up to the love and service of Jesus Christ. For the battery which the higher will sustains from the divine will on one side and the sensual will on the other, warring against it, is so sharp and violent that it entails much suffering.

Those who are experienced in the ways of virtue or vice do not feel this, but pursue the course they have entered upon with less difficulty; the virtuous yielding readily their will to the divine will, the vicious yielding without resistance to the will of the flesh.

But let no one suppose it possible to form true Christian virtues, and to serve God as he ought, unless he is ready in good earnest to do violence to his own inclinations, and to endure the pain of giving up all the things which pleased him, both great and small, and to which he had clung with earthly affection.

For this reason few reach perfection; for when they have overcome their greater faults with much toil, they will not continue to do violence to themselves, by bearing the vexation and weariness which the resistance of the countless little wishes and little movements of the passions involves. Thus these insignificant enemies are permitted to have their own way, and so to obtain complete mastery over their hearts. All those who, if they do not take what belongs to others, yet cling inordinately to that which is lawfully their own, are of this class. If they do not take unlawful measures for the sake of obtaining honors, yet they do not, as they should, shun them; but, on the contrary, they covet them, and even sometimes by various ways seek to gain them. If they keep the days of fasting, they do not mortify their appetite as to superfluities, nor as to the delicacies which they crave for. If they live chaste lives, yet they do not abstain from some indulgences which hinder much their union with God and their growth in the spiritual life, and which even to the holiest persons are dangerous, and are especially so to those who fear them least, and therefore should be avoided by all to the utmost of their power.

The result of this course is, that all other good works are done in a lukewarm spirit, are mixed up with much self-seeking and secret imperfections, and are accompanied by a certain self-esteem, and by a desire for the praise and appreciation of the world.

Such persons not only fail to advance in the way of salvation, but, by turning back, stand in danger of relapsing into their old sins; because they have no love for true virtue, and show little gratitude to the Lord who rescued them from the bondage of the devil. Moreover, they are too blind and ignorant to see their real danger, whilst they delude themselves with the idea that they are in a safe condition.

Here we discover a great error, and one so

much the more injurious as it is the less guarded against. Many who aspire to the spiritual life, being rather lovers of themselves than of that which is needful (altho indeed they know it not), select for the most part those practises which accord with their own taste, and neglect others which touch to the quick their natural inclinations and sensual appetites, to overcome which all reason demands that they should put forth their full strength.

Therefore, beloved, I advise and entreat you to cherish a love for that which is painful and difficult, for such things will bring you victory over self—on this all depends. That victory will be the more certain and speedy, the more resolutely you give your heart to those toils which in the path of piety and in war are the lot of beginners; and if you love the toil and hardship of the struggle, rather than the victory and the virtue, you shall the sooner gain all things

Of the Way to Resist the Sensual Impulses, and of the Acts to Be Performed By the Will, In Order to Acquire Habits of Virtue

Whenever the reasonable will is attracted by the will of the flesh on one side, and by the divine will on the other, each contending for the mastery, it will be necessary to exercise yourself in many ways, in order that the divine will may in all things prevail within you.

First, whenever you are assaulted and buffeted by the impulses of the lower nature, you must resist them manfully, so that the higher will may not consent.

Secondly, when the assaults have ceased, excite them again, so as to have an opportunity of overcoming them with greater force and energy. Then, challenge them again a third time, so as to accustom yourself to repulse them with scorn and horror. These two challenges to battle should be made in the case of every unruly appetite, with the exception of temptations of the flesh, of which we will treat in their place.

Lastly, you should make acts contrary to each evil passion you have to resist. You will understand this the better by the following example:

Suppose, then, you are attacked by feelings of impatience. Look well into yourself, and you will discover that the higher will is continually aimed at by these temptations, in order to incline it to consent to them. At once resort to the first thing which has been recommended; use the higher will repeatedly in opposing these feelings, resist them with all your might, that you may not be drawn to consent to them. Do not leave off the conflict till the enemy is, as it were, wearied out, dead, and yields himself up discomfited.

But, beloved, see the malice of the devil. When he perceives that we resolutely resist the rising of any passion, he not only refrains from stirring it, but when it is excited he seeks to quiet it for the time, lest, by the practise of resisting it, we should form the habit of the opposite virtue. And besides this, he would dexterously lead us to believe, that we have as brave soldiers quickly trampled under foot our enemies at one blow, so that he may entrap us into the snares of pride and vainglory.

Therefore, pass on from a first to a second encounter, by recalling to memory and exciting anew within you those thoughts which led to the temptation of impatience, until you are conscious of the feeling again; then resist with a stronger will than before, and with greater force repress the feelings.

And because, unless we thoroughly hate them, we are still in danger of being overcome by fresh attacks from our enemies—however successful we may have been in resisting them from a sense of duty and a desire to please God—you must face them a third time, and drive them far from you, not only with dislike but with disdain, picturing them to yourself as objects of hatred and abhorrence.

Lastly, in order that the soul may be adorned and perfected with habits of virtue, you must often make inward acts which are directly opposed to your unruly passions.

Thus, if you want to gain perfect patience, when you have received an affront which tempts to impatience, it will not be enough to exercise yourself in the three ways of fighting which I have already described, you must learn further to desire and love the slight you have received, wishing for a repetition of it, and from the same person; awaiting and disposing yourself to suffer still greater insults. These contrary acts are necessary for our perfection in holiness, because the above-named exercises of resistance—many and efficacious as they are—are not sufficient to pluck out the roots of sin.

And therefore (to continue the same instance) altho, on receiving an insult we may not consent to the feelings of impatience, but fight against them in the three ways which have been recommended; yet, unless we accustom ourselves by many and constant acts of the will to love contempt and rejoice in it, we shall never be free from the vice of impatience, springing as it does from a regard for our own reputation and a dread of contempt. And if the root of this sin be left alive, it will be sure to spring up afresh again and again, until virtue is weakened, and wholly choked by it; it will keep us in continual danger of a relapse upon every occasion. Therefore, without these contrary acts, the true habit of virtues can never be acquired.

And keep in mind also that these acts must be so frequently made as to be sufficient to destroy the sinful habit; for this habit, having been formed by repeated acts of sin, can only be removed by repeated acts of the opposite virtue, and thus a counter-habit of holiness be attained. Moreover, a greater number of good acts are required to form a habit of virtue than of evil acts to form a vicious habit; in that the former acts are not in alliance with our nature, which is corrupt, but the latter are always aided by it.

Again, I would add to all that has been said,

that if the virtue you are striving to acquire need it, you must perform the outward acts in conformity with the inward; as, for example, speaking gently and lovingly, and if possible rendering services to those who have in any way vexed and thwarted you.

And altho these acts—both inward and outward—are done, or seem to be done, with such weakness of spirit as to make them appear to be a most unwilling service, yet you must on no account fail to do them; because, however weak they may be, they will keep you strong and secure in the battle, and make easy before you the path to victory.

Stand on your guard, and be self-controlled, so as to be ready to resist every assault of the passions, not only such as are hot and violent, but also the slightest and the gentlest movement; for these latter open the way for the former, and thus habits of sin are afterward generated in us. It comes to pass, from the little care men take to root out of their hearts lesser desires, that after having conquered the stronger cravings of the same passion, many, when they least expect it, have been assaulted and vanquished by their old enemies more completely and fatally than at the first.

Be mindful, too, sometimes to mortify and check yourself in things which are lawful but not necessary; for, from such a course of discipline, many good results will follow. You will in this way dispose yourself more and more for victory over self in other things, you will gain strength and skill to struggle against temptations, you will avoid manifold devices of the devil, and perform a work very pleasing to the Lord.

Beloved, I speak plainly to you; if in the way which I have taught you, you will go on faithfully and constantly in these holy exercises for reforming and mastering yourself, then, I promise you, that you shall in a short time make much progress, and become really spiritual, and not in name only.

But in no other way, or course of discipline —however such may commend itself to you and be agreeable to your taste, yea, tho it may seem to unite you in secret converse with your Lord—can I assure you that you will attain any real virtue or holiness. For this does not consist in (as I told you in the first chapter) neither does it spring from exercises which are pleasant to us and which accord with our natural tastes, but it is the fruit of the crucifying of the flesh with all its actions, and the renewing of man by the practise of the virtues of the gospel, and the uniting him to his crucified Creator.

Depend upon it, that as habits of sin are produced by many and repeated acts of the higher will, yielding itself to the sensual appetite; so, on the other hand, habits of the virtues of the gospel are acquired by the performance of frequent and repeated acts of conformity to the divine will, as it calls us to the practise of different virtues from time to time.

For as our will can never become vicious or earthly, however fiercely assaulted or allured by the lower nature, unless it inclines toward or consents to the temptations; so, on the other hand, our will, however forcibly drawn and assailed by inspirations and divine grace, will never beccome virtuous or be united to God, so long as by inward, and it may be, outward acts, it does not suffer itself to be brought into conformity with his will.

What Ought to Be Done When the Higher Will Seems to Be Wholly Overcome and Stifled by the Lower Will, and by Its Enemies

If sometimes the higher will should seem to you powerless against the lower and its other enemies, because you do not feel that your will is effectually set against them, yet stand firm and do not leave off fighting; for you must regard yourself as victorious, until you can clearly see that you have given way. For since the higher will can act without the lower, so the higher can never be compelled by the lower to yield, however hot the assaults of the latter may be.

God has, in truth, given to the will such liberty and such power that, if all the senses, all evil spirits, and all the world were to conspire together, and with their combined strength to assault and oppress it, the will could still in spite of them will or will not whatever it liked with perfect freedom, and could assert itself when it liked, and as often as, for as long as, in what manner, and for whatever end, best pleased it.

And if these enemies should ever attack you and press you with such violence as almost to stifle your will, so as to leave you, as it were, no breath to make an act of the will against them; yet do not lose courage, nor throw down your arms, but in such a case make use of your tongue and defend yourself by saying—"I do not yield to you, I do not consent to you"; after the manner of one who has been grasped and thrown to the ground by an enemy leaping upon him, whom, when he is unable to thrust at him with the point of his sword, he contrives to strike with the hilt. And as he strives to spring backward so as to wound his enemy with the point of the sword, so do you retire into the consideration of yourself, the knowledge that you are nothing, and that you can do nothing. Then, putting your trust in God who can do all things, strike a blow at the passion which attacks you, and say: "Help me, O Lord; help me, my God; help me, Jesu, Son of Mary, that I may not yield to this."

You may also, if the enemy gives you time for it, call in your understanding to aid your will, and by the use of various considerations impart to the will fresh power and spirit against the enemy. Thus, for example, when you are in some persecution or trouble, and are so attacked by temptations to impatience that the will can not, or at least will not, stand up against them, you may proceed to encourage it by considering some points, such as the following:

First, consider that if you have brought upon yourself the evil under which you are suffering, you deserve to bear it; for, in such a case, every rule of justice requires you to bear patiently the punishment which you have yourself been the means of inflicting.

Secondly, if you are not to blame in this particular matter, think that there are many faults which you have committed, for which you have received no chastisement from God, nor have you punished yourself for them as you ought. And seeing that the divine mercy has changed the punishment of these faults, which should have been eternal, or at least should last for ages in another world, into this light affliction, ought you not to receive it willingly, or even thankfully?

Thirdly, if the thought should come that the penance is a long one in comparison with the offense against the divine Majesty—a thought which no one can ever lawfully indulge—you must remember that it is only through the strait gate of much tribulation that any can enter into the kingdom of heaven.

Fourthly, think that were it possible to enter by an easier way, the law of love would not allow you to dream of doing so, seeing that the Son of God, with all his friends and members, reached that kingdom by the road of thorns and crosses.

Fifthly, the chief thought upon which your mind should dwell in this and in all other temptations is the will of your God, who, for the love he has for you, takes unspeakable delight in every act of virtue and mortification which you, as his faithful and devoted soldier, perform in return for his love to you. And be thoroughly convinced of this, that the more unreasonable in itself the trouble is, and the more shameful on account of the person from

whom it comes and therefore to you the more
vexatious and difficult to be borne, so much
the more pleasing will you be to the Lord; if,
in things disordered in themselves and especially grievous to you, you can approve and
love his divine will and providence, by which
every event—however irregular it may seem
to be—is disposed after a most perfect rule
and order.

[Following chapters deal with the Soldier of Christ
and directions for overcoming special evils—Passion, Lust,
the Tongue, Mental Anxiety, etc.—and with "the Assaults
and Devices of the Devil."]

Of Certain Suggestions for Overcoming Our Evil Passions, and Gaining New Virtues

Altho I have already said so much of the
means whereby you may overcome self, and
adorn yourself with virtues, I will yet give
you some further cautions.

First, in your endeavors after holiness,
never be persuaded to adopt that routine of
spiritual exercises which divides the week so
as to set apart one day for one particular
virtue and another day for another; but let the
order of your warfare and exercises be, to
war against those passions which have been
always injuring you, and which still often at-

tack and injure you, and to adorn yourself
with the virtues which are opposite to them,
as perfectly as possible. For when you have
gained these virtues, you will have no difficulty in acquiring the rest, as occasion offers;
and occasions will present themselves, inasmuch as all the virtues are so interlinked one
with another, that you can not possess one
perfectly without having all the rest already,
as it were, on the threshold of your heart.

Secondly, never set a fixt time for the attainment of virtues, nor say that you will
gain them in so many days, weeks, or years;
but, as an infant or a newly enlisted soldier,
fight your way, and push forward toward
the summit of perfection. Do not ever stand
still, even for an instant; for to stand still
in the way of virtue and perfection, is not to
recover breath or courage, but to relapse and
grow feebler than before. By standing still,
I mean making yourself believe that you have
perfectly gained the virtue, and thus that you
need pay little attention to the occasions
which may call you to new acts of the
virtue, or to slight failures in it.

Therefore be vigilant, fervent, and careful,
so as not to miss the least opportunity of exercising a virtue. Embrace every occasion
which may lead to it, and especially those
which are most difficult, because acts which

are most difficult to be performed are those which most quickly and thoroughly establish the habit; therefore love those who offer you such opportunities. But flee those only, and that with rapid step, with all haste and diligence, which may lead to temptations of the flesh.

Thirdly, as to virtues which are wholly internal, such as love of God, contempt of the world, self-abasement, hatred of evil passions and sin, patience and meekness, love for all men, even for those who injure us, and such like; it is not necessary to attain to these by degrees, nor to mount with gradual rise to perfection in them, but strive at once to make each act as perfect as possible.

Fourthly, let your whole mind, desire, and heart be set upon, wish for, and long for nothing but to gain the victory over the passion against which you are struggling, and to form the opposite virtue. Be this your world, your heaven, your earth, your whole treasure; and all with the view of pleasing God. Whether you are eating or fasting, laboring or resting, watching or sleeping, at home or abroad, whether engaged in devotion or in manual labor, let your aim be to overcome and subdue this passion, and to gain the opposite virtue.

Fifthly, be the foe of all earthly pleasures

and gratifications, and in this way you will
weaken the power of all vices, which have
their root in the love of pleasure. Therefore,
when this is cut away by hatred of self, they
lose their vigor and force. For if whilst you
on the one hand fight against a particular in-
dulgence, and on the other attach yourself
to some earthly delight (tho it be only venial),
hard will be the battle and bloody, and the
victory rare and very uncertain.

Therefore bear in mind those divine utter-
ances: "He that loveth his life shall lose it,
and he that hateth his life in this world shall
keep it unto life eternal" (John 12:25).
"Brethren, we are debtors not to the flesh, to
live after the flesh. For if ye live after the
flesh ye shall die; but if ye through the spirit
do mortify the deeds of the body, ye shall
live" (Rom. 8:12).

Sixthly, my last advice is, that you should
make a general examination of conscience, and
a confession of sin, observing all that is re-
quireth for doing it well; so shall you be more
certain that you are in your Lord's favor,
from whom alone all graces and victories must
be looked for.

That Virtues Are to Be Gained by De-grees, by Exercising Ourselves In Their Gradual Formation, and That Our Attention Must First Be Given to One Step, and Then to Another

Altho the true soldier of Christ who aspires to the height of perfection should not assign limits to his progress, still there are some forms of spiritual fervor which need to be checked with a certain discretion, lest, being ardently embraced at first, they should be soon exhausted, and thus fail us in the middle of our course. Therefore, besides what has been said about moderation in external exercises, we must also learn that even interior virtues had better be acquired by degrees, and step by step; for in this way that which is small soon becomes great and abiding. Thus, for example, we should not as a rule practise patience in the high degree, which consists in rejoicing in afflictions and desiring them, before we have passed through the lower degrees of the virtue.

Neither do I advise you to endeavor to give your attention to all the virtues at once, but to one only, and afterward to others; for thus the habit of virtue is more easily and firmly rooted in the soul. If you are striving to acquire one particular virtue, you remember it more readily on all occasions; your mind, too, is sharpened by the discovery of new ways of and motives for cultivating it, and the will bends itself more easily and earnestly in the pursuit of it, than if it were occupied with many virtues at once. And with this uniform exercise, the acts which concern one single virtue are performed with less fatigue, in consequence of their resemblance to one another. The performance of one act facilitates the performance of the next, which is like unto it; and by this common likeness they make a deeper impression on us, the seat of the heart being already prepared and disposed for receiving those which are newly produced, having already made room for similar acts before.

These reasons have the greater force as it is quite certain that every one who practises himself in one virtue at the same time learns the exercise of the rest; and thus, through the inseparable bond which exists between them, when one virtue grows the rest increase with it, as rays proceeding from one and the same divine light.

Of the Means by Which Virtues Are Acquired, and of the Way We Should Use Them, Allowing Some Space of Time to One Virtue Only

To acquire virtues, besides all that has been said above, we need a large and generous mind; a will neither unstable nor remiss, but resolute and strong, with the certain persuasion that many hindrances and trials have to be overcome.

There are, moreover, particular inclinations and affections which we may gain by frequently considering how pleasing they are to God, how noble and excellent in themselves, and how profitable and necessary for us, for from them all perfection has its origin and end.

Each morning, then, make a stedfast resolve to exercise yourself in them according to the events which are likely to happen during the day; and often, as it passes, examine yourself in order to see whether you have kept your resolution or not, and renew it with fresh earnestness. And this should be done especially with regard to the particular virtue which we are endeavoring to acquire.

Let the examples of the saints, and our meditations and prayers on the life and passion of Christ (so needful in every spiritual exercise), be all applied principally to the virtue which we have made it our task to practise. Let the same be done on all occasions (as we shall presently explain more particularly), however different they may be from one another.

Let us take pains to accustom ourselves to interior and exterior acts of virtue, that we may be enabled to perform them with the same facility and readiness, as we did those which accorded with our natural will. And (as we have said elsewhere) the more contrary these acts are to the natural will, the more quickly will they produce the good habit in the soul.

The sacred words of the Holy Scriptures, uttered by the voice, or at least with the mind, and selected according to the occasion, have a wonderful power to aid us in this exercise. We ought therefore to keep such texts in readiness as bear upon the virtue we are practising, and let them be repeated during the day, especially whenever the opposite passion begins to assert itself.

Thus, for example, if we are trying to gain patience, we can use the following words, or others like them:

"My children, suffer patiently the wrath that is come upon you from God" (Baruch 4:25).

"The expectation of the poor shall not perish for ever" (Ps. 9:18).

"He that is slow to anger is better than the mighty; and he that ruleth his spirit than he that taketh a city" (Prov. 16:32).

"In your patience possess ye your souls" (Luke 21:19).

"Let us run with patience the race that is set before us" (Heb. 12:1).

For the same purpose we may say the following, or some similar short prayers:

"Oh! sufferings most precious, which make me like my Lord Jesus enduring the passion for me!"

"Oh! Only Life of my soul, will it ever come to pass that I could live in contentment amidst a thousand agonies for thy glory!"

"Happy should I be, if in the midst of the furnace of affliction I could still burn with the desire of enduring greater things!"

We should use these short prayers, or others like them, which help toward the attainment of virtues, and are calculated to cherish the spirit of devotion.

These short prayers are called ejaculations, because they are shot like darts or arrows toward Heaven.

They have a great effect upon us, in stirring us to virtue, and penetrate even to the heart of God, if they have, so to speak, these two wings—one, a true knowledge that God is pleased with such spiritual exercises; the other, a true and ardent desire after holiness with the sole end of pleasing His Divine Majesty.

That In the Exercise of Virtue We Must Advance With Continual Diligence

Amongst the things which are most important and necessary for the attainment of virtues, besides those already taught, this is to be borne in mind; that we must uninterruptedly press forward toward the end we have purposed; else, by only standing still, we turn back.

For as soon as we leave off acts of virtue, it follows of necessity that, by the violent inclination of the sensual appetite and the action of external objects, many unruly passions are excited in us which impair or destroy holiness; and, besides that, we lose many graces and gifts, which, if we had continued to press onward, we might have gained from the Lord. In this respect the spiritual traveler is unlike the one who performs an earthly journey, for the latter may rest without losing the ground he has gained, while with the former this would be impossible. There is another difference too between them: the weariness of the earthly traveler increases with the continuance of the bodily exertion, while, in the spiritual journey, the longer the traveler walks the more strength and vigor he gains. For by the habit of virtue, the lower nature, which by its rebellion at first makes the way rough and toilsome, is gradually weakened; while the higher nature, in which virtue resides, gets more firm and robust. Therefore, as we progress in holiness, the pain which we felt lessens, and a certain secret joy, which, by the divine working had intermingled with it, increases more and more.

In this way, by steadily going on from one virtue to another, we arrive at last at the summit of the mountain, where the perfected soul can work without weariness, nay, with pleasure and joyfulness; because, having now conquered and tamed its unruly passions, and having risen above all created things and above itself, it lives happily in the heart of the Most High, and there, sweetly laboring, finds its repose.

[The next chapters assert that as we must always continue in the Exercise of the Virtues, so we must not shun any Opportunity which offers itself for their Attainment; That we ought to regard as precious every Opportunity which is afforded us for the Acquisition of Virtues; and chiefly those which present the greatest Difficulties, and show how to avail ourselves of the various Occasions which present themselves for the Exercise of a single Virtue.]

The Path of Paradise

What Is the Nature of Our Heart, and How It Ought to Be Governed

Your heart was created by God for this end alone, to be loved and possest by him. And with this love you can make it do whatever you wish; and every thing, however difficult it might be, will in this manner become easy to you; therefore you must in the first place fix and establish the intention of your heart, so that outward actions may flow from inward. For, altho corporal penances, and all those exercises which chastise and afflict the flesh, are praiseworthy when used with discretion, and when adapted to the particular circumstances of each person, yet, if you use only such means as these, you will never gain a single virtue, but on the contrary vanity and the wind of vainglory; and all your labor will be lost, unless these outward exercises are animated and guided by right inward dispositions.

The life of man is nothing but a warfare and a continual temptation; and in consequence of this warfare, you must live in a state of watchfulness, and ever keep a guard over your heart, so that it may continue in peace and quietness. And if you should feel the movement of some sensual disquietude within you, you must be careful to quiet it instantly, stilling your heart, and not permitting it to turn aside or wander after any of these things. Do this as often as any cause of disquietude presents itself, whether in prayer, or at any other time, and know that when you have learned to act thus, then will you have learned to pray aright; but remember that all this must be done sweetly and gently. In short, the whole and principal business of your life must consist in continually quieting your heart, and never letting it go astray.

Of the Care We Should Have to Preserve a Peaceful Spirit

Therefore, above all things, you must be careful to place this sentinel of peace over all your feelings; it will lead you to great things without any toil, even with great tranquility and safety. And with this sentinel, which God has given you, you will so watch over yourself as to gain the habits of prayer, obedience, lowliness, and of bearing injuries without loss of composure.

It is very true that before you can attain to

this degree of peace, you will have to take
great pains through want of practise, but
afterward your soul will abide in a state of
great consolation, whatever contradiction may
befall it; and from day to day you will gain
more and more the power of preserving a
peaceful spirit. And if sometimes you feel
so disturbed and troubled as to be unable to
pacify yourself, have recourse at once to
prayer, and persevere in it, in imitation of
Christ our Lord, who prayed three times
in the garden, to give you an example that
prayer might be your only resource and refuge, and that, however sad and desponding
you may feel, you must not leave off praying,
until your will is conformed to the will of
God, and therefore has become devout and
calm, and also full of courage and fortitude,
so that it can accept and embrace that which
at first was an object of dread and abhorrence—going forth thus to greet it: "Arise,
let us be going; behold, he is at hand which
doth betray me."

How This Building of Inward Peace Must Be Gradually Constructed

Be careful, as I have before said, not to
permit any thing to disturb your heart, and
do not meddle with things which are likely to

disquiet it, but labor ever to keep it in peace; since in this way, the Lord will build up within your soul a city of peace, and your heart shall be a house of pleasures and delights. This only he asks of you, that when you feel agitated, you should begin again to quiet and calm yourself in all your actions and thoughts; for as a city is not built in a day, so neither must you think that this inward peace is to be acquired in a day, because this is nothing less than to build a house for the Lord, and a tabernacle for the Most High, making yourself his temple. And the Lord for whom it is built must himself be the Builder of it, otherwise your labor will be lost. Also consider that the grace of humility must be the entire foundation and main support of this work.

How the Soul Must Refuse All Consolation, for This Is True Humility and Poverty of Spirit, by Which This Peace of the Soul Is Acquired

If you would enter by this gate of humility (for there is no other entrance), you must toil and make every effort, especially in the beginning to embrace tribulations and adversity as your dear sisters—desiring to be despised by all, and to have no one who entertains a favorable opinion of you, or brings you comfort, but your God. Fix deeply in your heart the impression, that God alone is your God, your only Refuge, and that all things else are thorns to you, which will wound you if you press them to your heart. And if some affront is offered you, be very glad of it, and bear it with joy, being assured that, because of it, God is with you; and desire no other honor, and seek nothing else but to suffer for love of him, and whatever may redound to his greater glory. Strive to rejoice, when others use toward you injurious, reproachful, or contemptuous words; for a great treasure lies hid under the dust, and if you willingly accept it, you will soon find yourself rich, tho the one who has enriched you is unconscious of the benefit he has been the means of conferring upon you. Do not seek for the love or good opinion of any one in this life; that you may be left to suffer with Jesus crucified, and may have no one to hinder you. Be on your guard against yourself, as the greatest enemy you have. Do not follow your own will, your own disposition, your own judgment, if you would not destroy yourself. For this purpose you have need of arms to defend yourself from yourself; and when your will craves for any thing—however right the thing may be—always place it first, detached and naked and with deep humility, before your Lord, beseeching him that not your will but his may be done in it. And do this with desires wholly mortified, and without any admixture of self-love, knowing that you are nothing and can do nothing of yourself. Beware of your own opinions, which bear with them in appearance of sanctity and indiscreet zeal, against which the Lord cautions us: "Beware of false prophets, which come to you in sheep's clothing, but inwardly they are ravening wolves; by their fruits ye shall know them." Their fruits are the loss of inward peace and quietness. Every thing which separates you from humility, peace, and inward tranquility, in whatsoever dress or disguise it presents itself, is to you a false prophet, one of those who in sheep's clothing, that is, under the pretext of zeal, and of lending some indiscreet aid to your neighbor, are ravening wolves, which prey upon your humility and on that peace and quietness which are so necessary for all who seek real progress. And the greater the show of holiness in any thing, the more narrowly should it be examined; and this (as it has been before said) should be done in a spirit of repose and calmness. And if at times you should fail in something of this kind, be not disturbed, but humble yourself before your Lord, acknowledge your weakness, and learn a lesson for the future. Perhaps God has permitted you to fail, in order that he may bring down the pride which is still lurking within you, and you are not aware of it. If sometimes you feel your spirit pricked by some sharp and poisonous thorn, do not be disturbed because of it, but watch more diligently, lest it go further, and penetrate still more deeply. Withdraw your heart, and gently bring away your will into its abode of peace and quietness; keep your soul purely for God, whom you will ever find in your inmost parts and in the depth of your heart through the uprightness of your intention. Be assured that everything happens in order to prove you; and that in this way He may fit you for the good which is yours, and that you may be worthy of that crown of righteousness which by His Infinite Mercy is prepared for you.

How the Soul Should Be Kept In a State of Inward Solitude, That God May Work Therein

Set, then, very high value on your soul, since the Father of fathers, and Lord of lords, has created it for his own abode and temple. Esteem is so highly as never to suffer it to be degraded nor to incline to any other object. Let your desires and your hopes be ever directed toward the coming of your Lord, Who will not visit your soul unless it remains in solitude. Do not suppose, that in the presence of others he will open his lips, unless it be with words of reproach and abandonment. He wills that the soul shall be alone, having put aside, as far as may be, its own thoughts, its own desires, and, what is much more to the purpose, its own will. Yet you ought not to impose penances indiscreetly on yourself, nor go in quest of opportunities of suffering for the love of God, simply under the guidance of your own will; but only with the approval of some spiritual adviser, and of those who are over you, and who, under God, have the rule over you, for he, using them as his instruments, disposes your will to do whatever he wills, and in the way that he wills. You are not to do your own will, but to let God do in you what he wills. Let your will be always so freed from self as to have no desire of your own; and if you have a desire concerning any thing, desire it only in such a manner as not to feel regret, if you should be thwarted in it, but that your peace of mind may remain as undisturbed as if you had entertained no wish in the matter. This is true liberty of spirit, not to bind oneself to any thing. If you yield up your soul to God in this state of detachment, free and alone, you will see the wonders God will work in you. O wonderful solitude and secret chamber of the Most High, where only he will give audience, and speak to the inmost soul! O desert, thus made a paradise, since in it alone God vouchsafes to be seen, and to be conversed with! "I will turn aside, and see this great sight." But if you would come hither, enter barefoot upon this ground, for it is holy. First, put off your shoes from your feet, that is, the affections from your soul, and leave them bare and free; carry neither purse nor scrip for this road; for you must desire nothing in this world, whatever others may seek; neither salute any one; fix all your thoughts and affections upon God alone, and not on creatures; leave the dead to bury the dead; you go your way to the land of the living, and let death have no part with you.

Of the Prudence Which We Ought to Exercise In the Love of Our Neighbor, so as Not to Disturb This Peace

Experience itself will show you, if you will make trial of it, that this path of charity and love toward God and our neighbor is the most clear and plain road which leads to eternal life. The Lord said that he "came to send fire upon the earth," and that his only desire was "that it be kindled." But altho the love of God has no bounds, that for our neighbor should have; for, if it is not properly moderated, it might become a cause of great injury to you and lead you, through gaining others, to be lost and ruined yourself.

You must love your neighbor only in such a way as not to hurt you own soul. Altho you are bound to set a good example, yet you must not be actuated by that motive only, else you will lose all benefit to yourself. Act in all things with simplicity and piety, without respect to any thing but to please God alone. Be humble in all you do, and you will realize what little benefit the example of such an one as you are can be to others. Remember that your zeal and fervor for souls must not be such as to destroy your own quiet and peace. Have a burning thirst and longing that all others may know the truth which you know and understand, and be inebriated with that wine which God to each one promises and gives without price.

This thirst for the salvation of your neighbor you ought to have always; but it should take its source from your love for God, and not from your own indiscreet zeal. God must plant it in the solitude of your soul, and must gather the fruits of it when he wills. Sow nothing of yourself alone, but offer to God the ground of your soul, pure, and cleared of every thing, for then he will sow it with his own seed as he pleases, and so shall it yield fruit. Ever remember that God wills the soul to be alone and detached from all, that he may unite it to himself. Only allow him to choose you, and do not hinder him by your free-will. Sit without a thought of yourself, save that of pleasing God, waiting to be guided to what you have to do; for the Father of the family has already gone forth, and is seeking laborers. Lose all care and thought, strip off all anxiety about yourself and all affection for earthly things, so that God may clothe you with himself, and give you what is beyond your power to conceive. Forget yourself entirely, as much as possible, and let the love of God alone live in your soul. Of all that has been said, let this abide with you, that with all diligence (or, to put it better, with all diligence save that which disquiets) you must calm your zeal and fervor with great moderation, that so you may keep God within you, with all peace and tranquility, lest you lose the capital of your own soul, which is of the first importance, by indiscreetly putting it out to interest for the sake of others.

A silence, preserved in the way we have said, is a strong cry in the ear of God; idleness such as this turns everything to account, and is that which alone you must traffic with, if you would be rich toward God, for this is nothing else but to resign your soul to God, detached from all things. And this you must do without taking any credit to yourself, or imagining that you are doing something; for God does all, and on your side the Lord wills only that you should humble yourself in his sight and offer to him a soul, free and wholly detached from earthly things, with the inward desire that his divine will may be most perfectly, in all and through all, accomplished in you.

[The next chapters show how the Soul, despoiled of its own Will, must present itself before God ; and treat of the Faith we should have in the Most Holy Sacrament of the Altar ; and how we should Offer ourselves unto the Lord.]

That We Ought Not to Seek Pleasures, Nor the Things Which Gratify Our Tastes; But God Alone

Always choose toil, and love to be without the consolation of particular friendships and favors, which do not bring any profit with them to the soul; and rejoice to be ever subject to, and dependent on the will of others.

54

Let everything be a means of leading you to God, and let nothing detain you on the way. This should be your consolation, that every thing is bitter to you, and God your only repose. Let all your labors be directed to your Lord; love him, and give to him your whole heart without any fear; for he will find a good way to solve all your doubts, and will restore you when you fall. Lastly, in one word, if you will love him, you shall possess all good. Offer yourself to God for a sacrifice, in peace and quietness of spirit. And the better to advance in this journey, and to bear yourself up without weariness and vexation, you should at every step dispose your soul by expanding your will to the extent of the divine will; and the more your will is thus expanded, the more you will receive. Your will must be thus disposed, to will or not to will in every case according as God wills or does not will it. Always at every step renew your purpose of pleasing God, •and do not determine upon what course you will pursue, except for the passing moment, but for the future keep yourself free. No one, however, is forbidden to exercise a proper prudence and diligence in providing for necessaries, according to his position. For this is according to the will of God, and is no impediment to peace or genuine spiritual progress. Let your purpose be in all things to do your duty according to your ability, and be indifferent and resigned as to all results which are beyond you.

There is one thing always in your power, and that is to offer to God your will and desire no longer to will any thing of yourself; for as soon as you have this freedom, and are detached on all sides (which you can be always and everywhere, when occupied or not), you will enjoy tranquility and peace. In this freedom of spirit consists the great good which you have in view. This freedom is nothing else than the perseverance of the interior man within himself, without going forth to will, desire, or seek any thing out of himself; and all the time you abide in this state of liberty, you will rejoice in that divine servitude which is the great kingdom that is within us.

[The author then shows that the Servant of God must not be Discouraged, tho he feel within himself some Repugnance and Disquiet as to this Peace; discusses the Diligence which the Devil employs to Disturb this Peace, and how we ought to guard ourselves against his Devices; and shows that the Soul ought not to Disquiet itself on Account of Inward Temptation.]

That Temptations Are Sent Us by God for Our Good

To comprehend, then, more particularly, how it is that temptations are sent us by God for our good, we must consider that man, because of the evil inclinations of corrupt nature, is proud, ambitious, conceited, and always thinks himself to be more than he is. This self-esteem is so dangerous to true spiritual progress that the very scent of it is enough to hinder the attainment of perfection. Therefore our most faithful God, in that loving providence which he exercises over each one, and especially over those who have truly given themselves up to his service, takes care to place us in positions where we may escape so great a danger; so that we are as it were forced to come to a true knowledge of ourselves.

He acted thus with the Apostle Peter, permitting him to deny him, that thus he might know himself and no longer be self-confident; and with the Apostle Paul, who, after he had been caught up to the third heaven, and had heard divine secrets, was visited with a troublesome temptation, to the end that, knowing his natural weakness, he might remain humble, glorying only in his infirmities, and that the greatness of the revelations which God made to him should not lead him to presumption, as he himself says.

God, then, moved by compassion for our misery and perverse inclinations, permits these temptations to come upon us, and some-

times to be very horrible, and to come under
different forms, that we may humble ourselves and know ourselves, tho they seem to us
to be useless. It is in this way he manifests
his goodness and wisdom in making things
which seem to us most hurtful to be most
helpful, in that through them we become more
humble—which is the thing above all others
our souls need. For it generally happens that
the servant of God who is thus tried by
thoughts such as these, by indevotion and
dryness of spirit, concludes that they arise
from his own imperfections, and that there
can not be another soul so imperfect and so
lukewarm as his own; and he believes that
such thoughts come only to those who are
forsaken by God, and that he himself, therefore, deserves to be forsaken by him. It follows, then, that he, who once thought himself
to be something, is now brought, by this bitter
medicine, sent him from God, to regard himself as the most depraved person in the world
and as one unworthy to be called a Christian;
and he never would have arrived at this low
opinion of himself, nor attained to such a
depth of humility, had he not been sorely
tried and forced as it were to it by these extraordinary temptations.

There is one favor which God confers in
this life on the soul which has placed itself

back and given itself up into his hands, and that is, to give it whatever medicine he pleases, and to administer that which he in his perfect knowledge sees the soul stands in need of for its health and well-being.

Again, besides this fruit, which our souls gain from such trials as lack of devotion, there are many others; thus, he who is so afflicted, is as it were constrained to have recourse to God, and to seek to do good works, as a remedy for his distress; and in the same way, in order to free himself from such torture, he sets about examining his heart, avoiding all sin, and everything which seems to be imperfect, or which may in any way place him at a distance from God. And thus this trial, which in his judgment appeared to be so adverse and hurtful, served for a lash to make him run toward God with greater fervor, and keep away from everything which he thinks is not in conformity with the divine will. And in all these trials, all the toil and travail the soul endures braving these temptations and withdrawals of spiritual delights are, so to speak, but a loving purgatory, if they are borne with humility and patience; and they will help us to win that crown in heaven which otherwise we could not obtain, the glory of which will be in proportion to the toil and pain through which it was gained.

Hence we see how little ground there is for that discontent or alarm which inexperienced persons entertain, who attribute this trial to the devil or to their own sins and imperfections, when it comes to them from the hand of God.

Tokens of love they take as signs of hatred, and imagine that these divine favors and caresses are blows which come from an enraged heart, and believe that all they do is lost and worthless, and that this loss is irremediable. Whereas did they but rightly believe that not only vas there no loss, but great gain (if the soul properly used the opportunity, as it always has the power of doing), and that all was an evidence of God's loving remembrance of us; it would not be possible for them to be disquieted or to lose peace when they perceived themselves to be troubled with many temptations and imaginations, and found themselves dry and indevout in prayer and other exercises. On the contrary, they would with fresh perseverance humble their souls in the sight of the Lord, purposing in all and through all to accomplish the divine will in whatever manner the Lord may will to be served by them in this world; using diligence to keep themselves peaceful and tranquil, taking every thing from the hand of their Heavenly Father, in whose hand alone is the cup from which they have to drink.

For whether the trouble and temptation arise from the devil or from men, or on account of sins, or in whatever way, it is always God who gives it to you, tho it reaches you through various channels, as it pleases him; since it is only the evil of the pain which reaches you, and this is always ordered for your good. Tho, however, the evil of the fault itself—for example, an act of injury or insult committed by your neighbor—is contrary to his will, yet so far as you are concerned, he makes use of it for your benefit and salvation. Therefore, instead of giving way to sadness and discontent, you should give thanks with inward joy and gladness, doing every thing that lies in your power with perseverance and resolution, not losing time and with that the many and great rewards which God wills that you should gain by this opportunity which he presents to you.

[Finally, the author discusses the Remedy which we ought to use, so as not to be disquieted under Faults and Infirmities; and how the Soul, without Loss of Time, should recover Calmness and make Progress.]

A Prayer of Thomas Becon

O heavenly Father, who watchest always over thy faithful people, and mightily defendest them, so that they be harmless preserved, I most heartily thank thee that it hath pleased thy fatherly goodness to take care of me this night past. I most entirely beseech thee, O most merciful Father, to show the like kindness toward me this day, in preserving my body and soul; that I may neither think, breathe, speak, nor do anything that may be displeasing to thy fatherly goodness, dangerous to myself, or hurtful to my neighbor; but that all my doings may be agreeable to thy most blessed will, which is alway good; that they may advance thy glory, answer to my vocation, and profit my neighbor, whom I ought to love as myself; that, whensoever thou callest me hence, I may be found the child not of darkness but of light; through Jesus Christ our Lord. AMEN.

SELECTIONS FROM

The Private Devotions

OF

LANCELOT ANDREWES

LANCELOT ANDREWES

English preacher and theologian; born at Barking, 1555; died at Winchester House, Southwark, September, 26, 1626. He entered Pembroke Hall, Cambridge, in 1571, was graduated B.A., 1575, was ordained 1580, and became catechist at Pembroke; he was master of Pembroke from 1589 to 1605. He also held the living of St. Giles's, Cripplegate, and was prebendary of St. Paul's; he became chaplain to the queen and dean of Westminster in the latter part of Elizabeth's reign. Under James I. he was made bishop of Chichester in 1605, of Ely in 1609, and of Winchester in 1619. Andrewes was a member of the Hampton Court Conference, and his name heads the list of scholars appointed in 1607 to prepare the Authorized Version. His works are to be found in the "Library of Anglo-Catholic Theology" (11 vols., Oxford, 1841-54). He is best known, however, by his "Private Devotions," of which there are many editions. He is also the author of "Seventeen Sermons on the Nativity" (1887).

Launcelot Andrewes

Preparation for Prayer

I. TIMES OF PRAYER: Always (Luke 18:1).
Without ceasing (1 Thess. 5:17).
At all times (Eph. 6:18).

Samuel among such as call upon his name (Ps. 99:6).

God forbid that I should sin against the Lord in ceasing to pray for you, and showing you the good and the right way (1 Sam. 12:23).

We will give ourselves continually to prayer and to the ministry of the word (Acts 6:4).

He kneeled upon his knees three times a day, and prayed and gave thanks before his God, as he did aforetime (Dan. 6:10).

In the evening, and morning, and at noon day will I pray, and that instantly, and he shall hear my voice (Ps. 55:18).

Seven times a day do I praise thee (Ps. 119:164).

1. In the morning, a great while before day (Mark 1:35).

2. In the morning watch (Ps. 63:6; comp. also Ps. 130:6).

3. The third hour of the day (Acts 2:15).

4. About the sixth hour (Acts 10:9).

5. The hour of prayer, the ninth (Acts 3:1).

6. The eventide (Gen. 24:63).

7. By night (Ps. 134:2).

At midnight (Ps. 119:62).

II. PLACES OF PRAYER: In all places where I record my name, I will come to thee, and I will bless thee (Exod. 20:24).

Let thine eyes be open toward this house night and day, even toward the place of which thou hast said, my name shall be there; that thou mayest hearken unto the prayer which thy servant shall make toward this place (1 Kings 8:29).

Thou that hearest prayer, unto thee shall all flesh come. The fierceness of man shall turn to thy praise, and the fierceness of them shalt thou refrain. As for me, I will come into thy house, even upon the multitude of thy mercy, and in thy fear will I worship toward thy holy temple. Hear the voice of my humble petitions, when I cry unto thee; when I hold up my hands toward the mercy-seat of thy holy temple. We wait for thy loving kindness, O God, in the midst of thy temple.

1. Among the faithful, and in the congregation (Ps. 111:1).

2. Enter into thy closet, and when thou hast shut thy door, pray to thy Father which is in secret (Matt. 6:6).

3. They went up into an upper room (Acts 1:13).

4. He went up upon the housetop to pray (Acts 10:9).

5. They went up together into the Temple (Acts 3:1).

6. We kneeled down on the shore, and prayed (Acts 21:5).

7. He went forth over the brook Cedron, where was a garden (John 18:1).

8. Let them rejoice in their beds (Ps. 149:5).

9. He departed into a desert place, and there prayed (Mark 1:35).

10. In every place lifting up holy hands without wrath and doubting (1 Tim. 2:8).

III. CIRCUMSTANCES OF PRAYER:

1. Kneeling.

He kneeled down and prayed (Luke 22:41).

He went a little further, and fell on his face, and prayed (Matt. 26:39).

My soul is brought low, even unto the dust, my belly cleaveth unto the ground (Ps. 44:25).

2. Sinking the head, drooping the face (Ezra 9:6).

3. Smiting the breast (Luke 18:13).

4. Shuddering (Acts 16:29).

5. Groaning, clasping of hands (Isa. 59:11).

6. Raising of eyes and hands (Ps. 25:15; 143:6).

7. Blows (Ps. 73:14).

Order of Morning Prayer

LITANY: Glory be to thee, O Lord, glory to thee. Glory to thee who givest me sleep to recruit my weakness, and to remit the toils of this fretful flesh. To this day and all days, a perfect, holy, peaceful, healthy, sinless course,

Vouchsafe, O Lord.

The angel of peace, a faithful guide, guardian of souls and bodies, to encamp around me, and ever to prompt what is salutary,

Vouchsafe, O Lord.

Pardon and remission of all sins and of all offenses,

Vouchsafe, O Lord.

To our souls what is good and convenient, and peace to the world,

Vouchsafe, O Lord.

Repentance and strictness for the residue of our life, and health and peace to the end,

Vouchsafe, O Lord.

Whatever is true, whatever is honest, whatever just, whatever pure, whatever lovely, whatever of good report, if there be any virtue, if any praise, such thoughts, such deeds,

> Vouchsafe, O Lord.

A Christian close, without sin, without shame, and, should it please thee, without pain, and a good answer at the dreadful and fearful judgment-seat of Jesus Christ our Lord,

> Vouchsafe, O Lord.

CONFESSION: Essence beyond essence, Nature increate, Framer of the world, I set thee, Lord, before my face, and I lift up my soul unto thee. I worship thee on my knees, and humble myself under thy mighty hand. I stretch forth my hands unto thee, my soul graspeth unto thee as a thirsty land. I smite on my breast, and say with the publican, God be merciful to me a sinner, the chief of sinners; to the sinner above the publican, be merciful as to the publican. Father of mercies, I beseech thy fatherly affection, despise me not an unclean worm, a dead dog, a putrid corpse; despise not thou the work of thine own hands; despise not thine own image tho branded by sin. Lord, if thou wilt, thou canst make me clean; Lord only say the word, and I shall be cleansed. And thou my Savior Christ, Christ my Savior, Savior of sinners, of whom I am chief, despise me not; despise me not, O Lord, despise not the cost of thy blood, who am called by thy name; but look on me with those eyes with which thou didst look upon Magdalene at the feast, Peter in the hall, the thief on the wood; that with the thief I may entreat thee humbly. Remember me, Lord, in thy kingdom; that with Peter I may bitterly weep and say, O that mine eyes were a fountain of tears, that I might weep day and night; that with Magdalene I may hear thee say, Thy sins be forgiven thee, and with her may love much, for many sins, yea manifold, have been forgiven me. And thou, all-holy, good, and life-giving Spirit, despise me not, thy breath, despise not thine own holy things; but turn thee again, O Lord, at the last, and be gracious unto thy servant.

COMMENDATION: Blessed art thou, O Lord, our God, the God of our fathers; who turnest the shadow of death into the morning, and lightenest the face of the earth; who separatest darkness from the face of the light, and banishest night and bringest back the day; who lightenest mine eyes, that I sleep not in death; who deliverest me from the terror by night, from the pestilence that walketh in darkness; who drivest sleep from mine eyes,

and slumber from mine eyelids; who makest
the outgoings of the morning and evening to
praise thee; because I laid me down and slept
and rose up again, for the Lord sustained me;
because I waked and beheld, and my sleep
was sweet unto me. Blot out as a thick cloud
my transgressions, and as a cloud my sins;
grant me to be a child of light, a child of the
day, to walk soberly, holily, honestly, as in
the day; vouchsafe to keep me this day
without sin. Thou who upholdest the falling
and liftest the fallen, let me not harden my
heart in provocation or temptation or de-
ceitfulness of any sin. Moreover, deliver me
to-day from the snare of the hunter and
from the noisome pestilence; from the arrow
that flieth by day, from the sickness that
destroyeth in the noon day. Defend this day
against my evil, against the evil of this day
defend thou me. Let not my days be spent
in vanity, nor my years in sorrow. One day
telleth another, and one night certifieth
another. O let me hear thy loving-kindness
betimes in the morning, for in thee is my
trust; shew thou me the way that I should
walk in, for I lift up my soul unto thee. Deliver me, O Lord, from mine enemies, for I flee
unto thee. Teach me to do the thing that
pleaseth thee, for thou art my God; Let thy
loving spirit lead me forth into the land of

righteousness. Quicken me, O Lord, for thy name's sake, and for thy righteousness' sake bring my soul out of trouble; remove from me foolish imaginations, inspire those which are good and pleasing in thy sight. Turn away mine eyes lest they behold vanity; let mine eyes look right on, and let mine eyelids look straight before me. Hedge up mine ears with thorns, lest they incline to undisciplined words. Give me early the ear to hear, and open mine ears to the instruction of thy oracles. Set a watch, O Lord, before my mouth, and keep the door of my lips. Let my word be seasoned with salt, that it may minister grace to the hearers. Let no deed be grief unto me, nor offense of heart. Let me do some work for which thou wilt remember me, Lord, for good, and spare me according to the greatness of thy mercy. Into thine hands I commend my spirit, soul, and body, which thou hast created, redeemed, regenerated, O Lord, thou God of truth; and together with me all mine and all that belongs to me. Thou hast vouchsafed them to me, Lord, in thy goodness. Guard us from all evil, guard our souls, I beseech thee, O Lord. Guard us without falling, and place us immaculate in the presence of thy glory in that day. Guard my going out and my coming in henceforth and for ever. Prosper, I pray

thee, thy servant this day, and grant him
mercy in the sight of those who meet him.
O God, make speed to save me, O Lord, make
haste to help me. O turn thee then unto me,
and have mercy upon me; give thy strength
unto thy servant, and help the son of thine
handmaid. Shew some token upon me for
good, that they who hate me may see it and
be ashamed, because thou, Lord, hast holpen
me and comforted me.

Order of Evening Prayer

MEDITATION: The day is gone, and I give
thee thanks, O Lord. Evening is at hand,
make it bright unto us. As day has its
evening so also has life; the even of life is
age, age has overtaken me, make it bright
unto us. Cast me not away in the time of age;
forsake me not when my strength faileth me.
Even to my old age be thou he, and even
to hoar hairs carry me; do thou make, do thou
bear, do thou carry and deliver me. Abide
with me, Lord, for it is toward evening, and
the day is far spent of this fretful life. Let
thy strength be made perfect in my weakness.
Day is fled and gone, life too is going, this
lifeless life. Night cometh, and cometh death,
the deathless death. Near as is the end of
day, so too the end of life. We then also

remembering it, beseech of thee for the close of our life that thou wouldst direct it in peace, Christian, acceptable, sinless, shameless, and, if it please thee, painless, Lord, O Lord, gathering us together under the feet of thine Elect, when thou wilt, and as thou wilt, only without shame and sins. Remember we the days of darkness, for they shall be many, lest we be cast into outer darkness. Remember we to outstrip the night, doing some good thing.

Near is judgment—a good and acceptable answer at the dreadful and fearful judgment-seat of Jesus Christ vouchsafe to us, O Lord. By night I lift up my hands in the sanctuary, and praise the Lord. The Lord hath granted his loving-kindness in the daytime; and in the night season did I sing of him, and made my prayer unto the God of my life. As long as I live will I magnify thee in this manner, and I lift up my hands in thy name. Let my prayer be set forth in thy sight as the incense, and let the lifting up of my hands be an evening sacrifice. Blessed art thou, O Lord, our God, the God of our fathers, who hast created the changes of days and nights, who givest songs in the night, who hast delivered us from the evil of this day, who hast not cut off like a weaver my life, nor from day even to night made an end of me.

Confession: Lord, as we add day to day,

so sin to sin. The just falleth seven times a day; and I, an exceeding sinner, seventy times seven; a wonderful, a horrible thing, O Lord. But I turn with groans from my evil ways, and I return into my heart, and with all my heart I turn to thee, O God of penitents and Savior of sinners; and evening by evening I will return in the innermost marrow of my soul; and my soul out of the deep crieth unto thee. I have sinned, O Lord, against thee, heavily against thee; alas, alas, wo is me! for my misery. I repent, O me, I repent; spare me, O Lord; I repent, O me, I repent, help thou my impotence. Be appeased, spare me, O Lord; be appeased, have mercy on me; I said, Lord, have mercy upon me, heal my soul, for I have sinned against thee. Have mercy upon me, O Lord, after thy great goodness, according to the multitude of thy mercies do away mine offenses. Remit the guilt, heal the wound, blot out the stains, clear away the shame, rescue from the tyranny, and make me not a public example. O bring thou me out of my trouble, cleanse thou me from secret fault, keep back thy servant also from presumptuous sins. My wanderings of mind and idle talking lay not to my charge. Remove the dark and muddy flood of foul and wicked thoughts. O Lord, I have destroyed myself; whatever I have done amiss, pardon mercifully. Deal not with us after our sins, neither reward us after our iniquities. Look mercifully upon our infirmities; and for the glory of thy all-holy name, turn from us all those ills and miseries, which by our sins, and by us through them, are most righteously and worthily deserved.

COMMENDATION: To my weariness, O Lord, vouchsafe thou rest, to my exhaustion renew thou strength. Lighten mine eyes that I sleep not in death. Deliver me from the terror by night, the pestilence that walketh in darkness. Supply me with healthy sleep, and to pass through this night without fear. O keeper of Israel, who neither slumberest nor sleepest, guard me this night from all evil, guard my soul, O Lord. Visit me with the visitation of thine own, reveal to me wisdom in the visions of the night. If not (for I am not worthy—not worthy), at least, O loving Lord, let sleep be to me a breathing time as from toil, so from sin. Yea, O Lord, nor let me in my dreams imagine what may anger thee, what may defile me. Let not my loins be filled with illusions, yea, let my reins chasten me in the night season, yet without grievous terror. Preserve me from the black sleep of sin; all earthly and evil thoughts put to sleep within me. Grant to me light sleep, rid of all imaginations fleshly and satanical.

Lord, thou knowest how sleepless are mine unseen foes, and how feeble my wretched flesh, who madest me; shelter me with the wing of thy pity; awaken me at the fitting time, the time of prayer; and give me to seek thee early, for thy glory and for thy service. Into thy hands, O Lord, I commend myself, my spirit, soul, and body: thou didst make, and didst redeem them; and together with me, all my friends and all that belongs to me. Thou hast vouchsafed them to me, Lord, in thy goodness. Guard my lying down and my rising up, from henceforth and for ever. Let me remember thee on my bed, and search out my spirit; let me wake up and be present with thee; let me lay me down in peace, and take my rest: for it is thou, Lord, only, that makest me dwell in safety.

Prayers for a Week Day

INTRODUCTION: Through the tender mercies of our God the day-spring from on high hath visited us. Glory be to thee, O Lord, glory to thee. Creator of the light, and Enlightener of the world—of the visible light, the sun's ray, a flame of fire, day and night, evening and morning—of the light invisible, the revelation of God, writing of the law, oracles of prophets, music of psalms, instruction of

77

proverbs, experience of histories—light which never sets. God is the Lord who hath showed us light; bind the sacrifice with cords, yea even unto the horns of the altar.

O by thy resurrection raise us up unto newness of life, supplying to us frames of repentance. The God of peace, who did bring again from the dead the great Shepherd of the sheep, through the blood of the everlasting covenant, our Lord Jesus Christ, perfect us in every good work, to do his will, working in us what is acceptable before him, through Jesus Christ, to whom be glory for ever.

Thou who didst send down on thy disciples on this day thy thrice-holy Spirit, withdraw not thou the gift, O Lord, from us, but renew it in us, day by day, who ask thee for it.

CONFESSION: Merciful and pitiful Lord, long-suffering and full of pity, I have sinned, Lord, I have sinned against thee; O me, wretched that I am, I have sinned, Lord, against thee much and grievously, in attending on vanities and lies. I conceal nothing: I make no excuses. I give thee glory, O Lord, this day, I denounce against myself my sins. Truly I have sinned before the Lord, and thus have I done. I have sinned and perverted that which was right, and it profited me not. And what shall I now say? or with what shall I open my mouth? What shall I answer, seeing I have done it? Without plea, without defense, self-condemned am I. I have destroyed myself. Unto thee, O Lord, belongeth righteousness, but unto me confusion of face, because thou art just in all that is come upon me; for thou hast done right, but I have done wickedly. And now, Lord, what is my hope? Truly my hope is even in thee, if hope of salvation remain to me, if thy loving-kindness cover the multitude of my iniquities. O remember what my substance is, the work of thine hands, the likeness of thy countenance, the cost of thy blood, a name from thy name, a sheep of thy pasture, a son of the covenant. Despise not thou the work of thine own hands. Hast thou made for naught thine own image and likeness? for naught, if thou destroy it. And what profit is there in my blood? Thine enemies will rejoice; may they never rejoice, O Lord! Grant not to them my destruction. Look upon the face of thine Anointed, and in the blood of thy covenant, the propitiation for the sins of the whole world, Lord, be propitious unto me, a sinner; even unto me, O Lord, of sinners chief, chiefest and greatest. For thy name's sake be merciful unto my sin, for it is great: it exceeds. For thy name's sake—that name, beside which, none other under heaven is given among men whereby we must be saved, the Spirit himself helping our infirmities, and making intercession for us with plaints unutterable. For the tender yearnings of the Father, the bloody wounds of the Son, the unutterable plaints of the Spirit, give ear, O Lord, have mercy, O Lord, hearken and do; defer not, for thine own sake, O my God. For me, I forget not my sins, they are ever before me; I remember them in the bitterness of my soul; I am anxious about them; I turn away and groan, I have indignation and revenge and wrath against myself. I despise and bruise my own self, that my penitence, Lord, O Lord, is not deeper, is not fuller; help thou mine impenitence. And more, and still more, pierce thou, rend, crush my heart; and remit, forgive, pardon what things are grief to me and offense of heart. Cleanse thou me from secret faults, and keep thy servant also from presumptuous sins. Magnify thy mercies toward the wretched sinner; and in season, Lord, say to me, Be of good cheer; thy sins are forgiven thee; my grace is sufficient for thee. Say unto my soul, I am thy salvation. Why art thou so heavy, O my soul? and why art thou so disquieted within thee? Return unto thy rest, O my soul, for the Lord hath rewarded thee. O

Lord, rebuke me not in thine indignation, neither chasten me in thy displeasure. I said, I will confess my sins unto the Lord, and so thou forgavest the wickedness of my sin. Lord, thou knowest all my desire, and my groaning is not hid from thee. Have mercy upon me, O God, after thy great goodness, according to the multitude of thy mercies do away mine offenses. Thou shalt arise, and have mercy on me, O Lord, for it is time that thou have mercy upon me, yea, the time is come. If thou, O Lord, shouldst mark iniquities, O Lord, who shall stand? Enter not into judgment with thy servant, O Lord, for in thy sight shall no man living be justified.

PRAYER FOR GRACE: My hands will I lift up unto thy commandments which I have loved. Open thou mine eyes that I may see, incline my heart that I may desire, order my steps that I may follow the way of thy commandments. O Lord God, be thou to me a God, and beside thee none else, none else, naught else with thee. Vouchsafe to me to worship thee and serve thee (1) in truth of spirit; (2) in reverence of body; (3) in blessing of lips; (4) in private and in public; (5) to pay honor to them that have the rule over me, by obedience and submission; to show affection to my own, by carefulness and

providence; (6) to overcome evil with good;
(7) to possess my vessel in sanctification and
honor; (8) to have my converse without
covetousness, content with what I have; (9)
to speak the truth in love; to be desirous not
to lust, not to lust passionately, not to go after
lusts.

PROFESSION: I believe, O Lord, in thee,
Father, Word, Spirit, one God; that by thy
fatherly love and power all things were
created; that by the goodness and love to man
all things have been begun anew in thy Word,
who for us men and for our salvation, was
made flesh, was conceived and born, suffered
and was crucified, died and was buried, de-
scended and rose again, ascended and sat
down, will return and will repay; that by the
shining forth and working of thy Holy Spirit
a peculiar people hath been called out of the
whole world into a polity, in belief of the
truth and sanctity of living: that in it we
are partakers of the communion of saints
and forgiveness of sins in this world, that in
it we are waiting for resurrection of the flesh
and life everlasting in the world to come.
This most holy faith which was once delivered to the saints I believe, O Lord;
help thou mine unbelief, and vouchsafe
to me to love the Father for his fatherly love,
to reverence the Almighty for his power, as

a faithful Creator, to commit my soul to
him in well doing; vouchsafe to me to partake
from Jesus of salvation, from Christ of
anointing, from the Only-Begotten of adoption; to worship the Lord for his conception
in faith, for his birth in humility, for his
sufferings in patience and hatred of sin, for
his cross to crucify beginnings, for his death
to mortify the flesh, for his burial to bury
evil thoughts in good works for his descent to
meditate upon hell, for his resurrection upon
newness of life, for his ascension to mind
things above, for his sitting on high to mind
the good things on his right, for his return
to fear his second appearance, for judgment
to judge myself ere I be judged. From the
Spirit vouchsafe me the breath of salutary
grace. In the Holy Catholic Church to have
my own calling, and holiness, and portion,
and a fellowship of her sacred rites and
prayers, fastings and groans, vigils, tears,
and sufferings, for assurance of remission of
sins, for hope of resurrection and translation to eternal life.

INTERCESSION: O hope of all the ends of
the earth, and of them that remain in the
broad sea; O thou on whom our fathers hoped,
and thou didst deliver them; on whom they
waited, and were not confounded; O my hope
from my youth, from my mother's breasts,

on whom I have been cast from the womb, be
thou my hope now and evermore, and my
portion in the land of the living: in thy
nature, in thy names, in thy types, in word
and in deed my hope, let me not be disappointed of my hope. O the Hope of all the
ends of the earth, remember thy whole creation for good, visit the world in thy compassion; O Guardian of men, O loving Lord,
remember all our race. Thou who hast shut
up all in unbelief, on all have pity, O Lord.
O thou who didst die and rise again, to be
Lord both of the dead and living, live we or
die we, thou art our Lord; Lord, have pity on
living and dead. O Helper of the helpless,
seasonable Aid in affliction, remember all who
are in necessity, and need thy succor. O God
of grace and truth, establish all who stand
in truth and grace, restore all who are sick
with heresies and sins. O wholesome Defense
of thine anointed, remember thy congregation
which thou hast purchased and redeemed of
old. O grant to all believers one heart and one
soul. Thou that walkest amid the golden
candlesticks, remove not our candlestick out
of its place. Amend what are wanting, establish what remain, which thou art ready to cast
away, which are ready to die. O Lord of the
harvest, send forth laborers, made sufficient
by thee, into thy harvest. O Portion of those

who wait in thy temple, grant to our clergy, rightly to divide the word of truth, rightly to walk in it; grant to thy Christian people to obey and submit to them. O King of nations, unto the ends of the earth, strengthen all the states of the inhabited world, as being thy ordinance, tho a creation of man. Scatter the nations that delight in war, make wars to cease in all the earth. O Expectation of the isles and their hope, Lord, save this island, and all the country in which we sojourn, from all affliction, peril, and need. Lord of lords, ruler of rulers, remember all rulers to whom thou hast given rule in the earth, and O remember specially our divinely guarded king, and work with him more and more, and prosper his way in all things. Speak good things unto his heart, for thy Church, and all thy people, grant to him profound and perpetual peace, that in his tranquility we may lead a quiet and peaceful life in all godliness and honesty. O thou by whom are ordained the powers that be, grant to those who are chief in court to be chief in virtue and thy fear; grant to the parliament thy holy wisdom; to our great men, to do nothing against but for the truth; to the courts of law, thy judgment, to judge in all things concerning all without preference, without partiality. O God of armies, give a prosperous course and strength to all the Christian army against the enemies of our most holy faith. Grant to our population to be subject unto the higher powers, not only for wrath, but also for conscience sake. Grant to farmers and graziers good seasons; to the fleet and fishers fair weather; to tradesmen, not to overreach one another; to mechanics, to pursue their business lawfully, down to the meanest workman, down to the poor. O God, not of us only but of our seed, bless our children among us, to advance in wisdom as in stature and in favor with thee and with men. Thou who wouldst have us provide for our own, and hatest the unnatural, remember, Lord, my relations according to the flesh; grant me to speak peace concerning them, and to seek their good. Thou who willest us to make return to our benefactors, remember, Lord, for good all from whom I have received good; keep them alive that they may be blest upon earth, and deliver them not into the will of their enemies. Thou who hast noted the man who neglects his own as worse than an infidel, remember in thy good pleasure all those in my household. Peace be to my house, the Son of peace upon all in it. Thou who wouldst that our righteousness exceed the righteousness of sinners, grant me, Lord, to love those who love me; my own friend, and my father's friend, and my friend's children, never to forsake. Thou who wouldst that we overcome evil with good and pray for those who persecute us, have pity on mine enemies, Lord, as on myself; and lead them together with me to thy heavenly kingdom. Thou who grantest the prayers of thy servants one for another, remember, Lord, for good, and pity all those who remember me in their prayers or whom I have promised to remember in mine. Thou who acceptest diligence in every good work, remember, Lord, as if they prayed to thee, those who for any good reason give not time to prayer. Arise, and have mercy on those who are in the last necessity, for it is time that thou hadst mercy upon them, yea, the time is come. Have mercy, on them, O Lord, as on me also, when in extremities. Remember, Lord, infants, children, the grown, the young, the middle-aged, the old, hungry, thirsty, naked, sick, prisoners, foreigners, friendless, unburied, all in extreme age and weakness, possest with devils and tempted to suicide, troubled by unclean spirits, the hopeless, the sick in soul or body, the weak-hearted, all in prison and chains, all under sentence of death: orphans, widows, foreigners, travelers, voyagers, women with child, women who give suck, all in bitter servitude, or mine, or galleys, or in

loneliness. Thou, Lord, shalt save both man
and beast, how excellent is thy mercy, O God!
And the children of men shall put their trust
under the shadow of thy wings. The Lord
bless us and keep us, and show the light of his
countenance upon us, and be merciful unto
us; the Lord lift up his countenance upon us,
and give us peace! I commend to thee, O
Lord, my soul and my body, my mind and my
thoughts, my prayers and my vows, my senses
and my limbs, my words and my works, my
life and my death; my brothers and my sisters
and their children; my friends, my benefactors, my well wishers, those who have a
claim on me; my kindred and my neighbors,
my country and all Christendom. I commend
to thee, Lord, my impulses and my startings,
my intentions and my attempts, my going
out and my coming in, my sitting down and
my rising up.

PRAISE: Up with our hearts; we lift them
to the Lord. O how very meet, and right,
and fitting, and due, in all and for all, at all
times, places, manners, in every season, every
spot, everywhere, always, altogether, to remember thee, to worship thee, to confess to
thee, to praise thee, to bless thee, to hymn
thee, to give thanks to thee, Maker, Nourisher,
Guardian, Governor, Preserver, Worker, Per-
fecter of all, Lord and Father, King and God,

Fountain of life and immortality, Treasure of
everlasting goods; whom the heavens hymn
and the heaven of heavens, the angels and all
the heavenly powers, one to other crying continually—and we the while, weak and unworthy, under their feet—Holy, Holy, Holy,
Lord God of Hosts; full is the whole heaven,
and the whole earth, and the majesty of thy
glory. Blessed be the glory of the Lord out
of his place, for his Godhead, his mysterious-
ness, his height, his sovereignty, his almighti-
ness, his eternity, his providence. The Lord
is my strength, my stony rock, and my defense, my deliverer, my succor, my buckler,
the horn also of my salvation and my refuge.

On Human Frailness

Have mercy on me, Lord, for I am weak;
remember, Lord, how short my time is; remember that I am but flesh, a wind that passeth
away, and cometh not again. My days are as
grass, as a flower of the field; for the wind
goeth over me, and I am gone, and my place
shall know me no more. I am dust and ashes,
earth and grass, flesh and breath, corruption
and the worm, a stranger upon the earth,
dwelling in a house of clay, few and evil my
days, to-day, and not to-morrow, in the morning, yet not until night, in a body of sin, in a

world of corruption, of few days, and full of
trouble, coming up and cut down like a flower,
and as a shadow having no stay. Remember
this, O Lord, and suffer, remit; what profit is
there in my blood, when I go down to the pit?
By the multitude of thy mercies, by the riches
and excessive redundance of thy pity, by all
that is dear to thee, all that we should plead,
and before and beyond all things, by thyself,
by thyself, O Lord, and by thy Christ, Lord,
have mercy upon me, the chief of sinners. O
my Lord, let thy mercy rejoice against thy
judgment in my sin. O Lord, hear; O Lord,
forgive; O Lord, hearken; O Lord, hearken
and do; do and defer not for thine own sake;
defer not, O Lord, my God.

An Act of Thanksgiving

Let all thy works praise thee, O Lord, and
thy saints give thanks unto thee. It is a good
thing to give thanks unto the Lord, and to sing
praises unto thy name, O Most High; to tell
of thy loving-kindness early in the morning,
and of thy truth in the night-season. I will exalt thee, my God, O King, and praise thy
name for ever and ever. Every day will I
give thanks unto thee and praise thy name
for ever and ever. Who didst call the
things that were not as tho they were; by

whom all things were made in heaven and in
earth, visible and invisible; who upholdest all
things by the word of thy power; who dost
not leave thyself without witness, in that thou
doest good, and givest us rain from heaven,
and fruitful seasons, filling our hearts with joy
and gladness; in that all things continue this
day according to their ordinance; for all
things serve thee; who, having before taken
counsel didst thyself, with thine own hands,
make man out of the dust of the earth, and
didst breathe into his nostrils the breath of
life, and didst honor him with thine image,
and didst charge thine angels concerning him,
and didst set him over the works of thine
hands, and didst place him in a paradise of
pleasure; and didst not despise him, even
when he despised thy law, but didst open for
him the door unto repentance and life, giving
him thy great and precious promise concerning the seed of the woman; who hast instructed
our race, by that which may be known of God,
by that which is written in the law, by the rite
of sacrifices, by the oracles of the prophets,
by the melody of the psalms, by the wisdom of
the proverbs, by the experience of the histories; who, when the fulness of time was come,
didst send forth thy Son, who took the seed of
Abraham, and made himself of no reputation,
putting on the form of a servant; and being

made of a woman, made under the law, by the oblation of his life accomplished its obedience, by the sacrifice of his death removed its curse; redeeming our race by his passion, quickening it by his resurrection; leaving nothing undone, that could be done, to make us partakers of the divine nature; who hath manifested in every place the savor of his knowledge by the preaching of the gospel; bearing himself witness with divers signs and wonders, by marvelous holiness of life, by mighty power even unto shedding of blood, by the incredible conversion of the world to the faith without assistance of authority, without intervention of persuasion; who hast made us children of the saints, and heirs of the same vocation; who hast granted to thy Church that she should be the pillar and ground of the truth; and that the gates of hell should not prevail against her; who hast granted unto our Church that she should keep that which was committed unto her, and should teach us the way of peace; who hast confirmed the throne of thy servant, our king; who makest peace in our borders, and fillest us with the flour of wheat; who hast made fast the bars of our gates, and hast blest our children within us; who hast clothed our enemies with confusion; who givest us everlasting felicity, and makest us glad with the

joy of thy countenance; who hast informed
our princes, and taught our senators wisdom;
who hast given us pastors according to thine
heart, that feed us with knowledge and understanding; who hast turned our swords into
plow-shares, and our spears into pruning-
hooks; who hast caused that there should be
no decay, no leading into captivity, and no
complaining in our streets; who didst bring
me forth into life, and didst bring me on to
the laver of regeneration, and renewing of
the Holy Ghost; and hast made known to me
thy ways; and hast winked at my sins, because
I should amend (Wisd. of Sol. 11:23), who
hast not shut me up in the hand of mine
iniquity, waiting to show mercy upon me; who
hast not suffered my heart to be hardened;
but hast left me compunction of soul, remembrance of my latter end, conscience of committed sins; who hast opened to me a gate of
hope, while I confess and implore, through the
power of thy mysteries and the keys; who hast
not cut off, like a weaver, my life, nor made
an end of me from day even to night; nor
taken me away in the midst of my days; but
hast holden my soul in life, and hast not suffered my feet to slip.

The Lord's Prayer Paraphrased

1. Let thy name be invoked by us; be thou our shield, and our exceeding great reward; whatever word proceedeth from thee, let it not be in us to say against it either good or bad. Give us bread to eat, and raiment to put on, and now forgive the sin and injustice of thy servants; and let us not take our own thought in our hearts on the day for the morrow, O Lord; and let not evils take hold on us.

2. Let thy name be blessed, now and evermore; give us not, for the wickedness of the people, into the hands of hypocritical rulers; let it be unto us, O Lord, as thou shalt will; let not thistles grow instead of wheat, and cockle instead of barley. I have sinned: what shall I do unto thee, O thou Keeper of men? I will make a covenant with my senses, that I may not even think upon evil. Six times deliver me from straits; and the seventh let not evil touch me.

3. Holiness unto the Lord: let us be unto thee a royal priesthood; let us go out and come in according unto thy mouth; let us not live by bread alone, but by every word which proceedeth out of thy mouth; take away our transgressions, iniquities, and sins; lead us not into temptation, not into bitterness; from the

destroying angel and every hurtful stroke, Good Lord, deliver us!

4. Blessed be the name of the Lord, henceforth, world without end, from the rising up of the sun unto the going down of the same; be thou our Hope, and our Portion in the land of the living; teach us to do the thing that pleaseth thee, for thou art our God; let thy loving Spirit lead us forth into the land of righteousness; the eyes of all wait upon thee, O God, that thou mayest give them their meat in due season; open thou thine hand, and fill all things living with plenteousness; have mercy upon us, O God, after thy great goodness; according to the multitude of thy mercies do away our offenses; let not the enemy prevail against us; neither the son of wickedness approach to hurt us; let no evil befall us, neither any plague come nigh our dwelling.

5. Let thy name be our strong tower, into which we may run and be safe; through thee kings reign; their hearts are in thy hand, and thou turnest them as the rivers of water; O Lord, turn them unto good. Let there not be a multitude of thoughts in our heart; but thy counsel, O Lord, let that stand. Two things have I asked of thee: deny them not to me before I die: give me neither poverty nor riches; feed me with food convenient for me. Who can confidently say, I am clean from my

sin? Be merciful unto thy servants, who have sinned against thee, and heal thou their souls; remove my path far from an occasion of sinning; and let me not approach to the doors of the house thereof; send not unto us a cruel messenger; but remove all evil far from our houses.

6. Let not thy name be evil spoken of through us among the heathen; let all nations and kings that will not serve thy kingdom come to an end; yea let them be utterly laid waste; let all thy counsel stand, and all that thou hast decreed come to pass; give seed to the sower, and the staff of life for our food; be not wroth with us very sore, and remember not our sins for ever; behold, look, we are all thy people; let us not put the stumbling-block of our iniquity before our face (Ezek. 14:4); set not thy face against us for evil.

7. Our Father, holy art thou; holy is thy name above every name; to be reverenced and hallowed of all, but of some more than others, and of me more than any. Yet have I not done so, nor attempted thereto what in me lay. Wo is me! that I have not; I confess it openly. I grieve from my heart, mind, soul, spirit; suppliant I ask for pardon, suppliant for grace, that henceforward I may so speak, do, live, that thy name by me may be hallowed, yea, and would that by others through me!

Thy kingdom, the end of my wishes, that I may come to it in the state of glory, come to me in the state of grace; in thy earthly kingdom, by thy grace, let me so perform something as that I may attain to a place in thy heavenly kingdom, tho the lowest at the feet of thy saints. Let the will of the flesh and of the man depart from me; let thy holy, just, and gracious will be done in the earth and by the earth (which I am) as it is in heaven. Give us what pertaineth to health, peace, and sufficiency, give us angels' bread unto life eternal. Forgive me my debts, my huge sum of debts, my foul backslidings, my frequent relapses, my daily wallowings. To thee, O Lord, justice, and to me confusion of face. My destruction cometh from myself. If thou, Lord, wert extreme to mark what is done amiss, O Lord, who may abide it? But with thee there is mercy, with God redemption; with God is plenteous redemption from sin; and he shall deliver from all iniquities; deliver me, Lord, from mine; deliver my soul from the nethermost hell. Deep crieth unto deep, that it may deliver from the deep. Other things also there be which I feel less, but which be not of less weight, perchance of greater, concerning which I ask for illumination, that I may be able to confess them. And lead me not, nor suffer me to be led, nor suffer me to fall into temptation, mindful of my weakness, and pitying it, and of my so often proved infirmity. But deliver me from evil: evil in myself, the flesh, and its temptation, evil in the devil, and his suggestions, evil in the punishments which most righteously and justly I have deserved, evil in the world to come—spare me there—afflict, O Lord, if needs, and wound me here; evil in the present world; spare me also in this; evil in this world, and its accidents; evil in the disease wherewith I struggle; evil in the business in which I am engaged; evils past, present, and to come —from all these things set me free, O Lord, and preserve me, thy servant, for evermore, even tho the last among the last. I beseech thee, O Lord, according to all thy mercy, let thy most righteous indignation be turned from me; for most grievously, and often, most often and grievously, have I sinned against thee; and especially forgive my latest and freshest sins against thee. Let thine anger be turned away from me, from my parents, brothers, and sisters, from my bishop and household, from my relations, friends, neighborhood, country, from all Christian peoples. AMEN.

Before Going to Church

But I will come unto thy house in the multitude of thy mercies; and in thy fear will I worship toward thy holy temple. Hear, O Lord, the voice of my prayer, when I cry unto thee, when I stretch forth my hands toward the mercy-seat of thy holy temple. We wait for thy loving-kindness, O God, in the midst of thy temple. Remember, O Lord, our brothers that are standing around us, and praying with us at this holy hour, for their zeal and devotion; remember them also who on reasonable causes are absent, and pity them and us according to the multitude of thy loving-kindnesses, O Lord. Lord, I have loved the habitation of thy house, and the place where thine honor dwelleth: that I may hear the voice of thanksgiving, and tell of all thy wondrous works. One thing I have desired of the Lord, which I will require, even that I may dwell in the house of the Lord all the days of my life, to behold the fair beauty of the Lord, and to visit his temple. My heart hath talked of thee: Seek ye my face; thy face, Lord, will I seek. Open me the gates of righteousness; that I may go into them, and give thanks unto the Lord.

A Prayer of Bernhard Albrecht

O thou God of peace, unite our hearts by thy bond of peace, that we may live with one another continually in gentleness and humility, in peace and unity. O thou God of patience, give us patience in the time of trial, and stedfastness to endure to the end. O thou Spirit of prayer, awaken our hearts, that we may lift up holy hands to God, and cry unto him in all our distresses. O thou gentle Wind, cool and refresh our hearts in all heat and anguish. Be our defense and shade in the time of need, our help in trial, our consolation when all things are against us. Come O thou eternal Light, Salvation, and Comfort, be our light in darkness, our salvation in life, our comfort in death; and lead us in the straight way to everlasting life, that we may praise thee forever. AMEN.

SELECTIONS FROM

A Treatise on the Love of God

INCLUDING

On the Union of the Soul With God

AND

Introduction to the Devout Life

BY

FRANCIS OF SALES

FRANCIS OF SALES

Saint and writer of the Roman Catholic Church; born at the Château de Sales near Annecy in Savoy, August 21, 1567; died at Lyons, December 28, 1622. At the age of twelve he entered the Jesuit college in Paris, where he studied philosophy, the classics, and Hebrew, leading at the same time a life of stern self-denial. From 1584 to 1590 he studied civil and canon law at Padua, but gave himself up more and more to theology under the guidance of the Jesuit Possevin. During a severe illness he determined to enter the priesthood, and carried out his purpose in 1591, in spite of the opposition of his family. In 1594 he was sent to the province of Chablais and to the district of Gex, lying on Lake Geneva. This region had become Calvinistic and his aim was to bring back to the Roman faith the inhabitants of that district. In 1602, on the death of the bishop of Geneva, Francis succeeded to the see, of which he had for some time been coadjutor. In 1618 Francis composed his famous "Introduction à la vie dévote," which has been translated into almost every language in Europe. Several of his works have appeared in English, *e.g.*, "Practical Piety" (London, 1851); "Spiritual Letters" (or selections from them, London, 1871); "Spiritual Conferences" (London, 1862); "Introduction to a Devout Life" (Oxford, 1875); "The Love of God" (London, 1902).

Of the Exercise of Divine Love in Prayer

A Definition of Prayer, or Mystical Theology

There are two ways of exercising our love for God: one affective, the other effective, and as St. Bernard calls it, active. By the first, we place our affections in God, and all that he loves becomes interesting to us; by the second we serve God, and accomplish what he ordains. The former unites us to the goodness of God; the latter renders us submissive to his holy will. By the one a kind of correspondence is established between us and God, by the communication of his spirit to our souls, and hence arise sentiments of complacency, of benevolence, transports, ecstacies, desires, sighs, and spiritual ardors; the other imparts solidity to our resolutions and an inviolable fidelity to our obedience, which enables us to accomplish the will of God—to suffer, to accept and embrace every thing that he pleases to order. By the first our happiness and delight are centered in God, and by the second we please and obey him. Affective love conceives the work, if I may say so, and effective love brings it forth. By the

By kind permission of Longmans, Green & Co., New York.

former we put the Almighty as a seal upon
our heart, or rather as a banner under which
all the affections of the soul are ranged
(Song of Songs, 8:6); by the latter we place
God upon our arm, as a sword to enable us
to perform exploits of spiritual valor, in the
practise of virtue. Effective love is principally exercised in prayer, wherein the emotions
of the heart are so multiplied and varied that
it is impossible to distinguish them all, not
only on account of their being very numerous,
but also because they are spiritual and consequently so imperceptible as to escape the
penetration of the mind. The best trained
dogs are liable to be at a fault, and to lose the
track of the stag; for its cunning teaches it a
thousand stratagems and subtleties, by which
it gives the hounds a wrong scent and thereby
escapes their pursuit. In the same manner,
we often lose sight of our own heart, and are
totally incapable of understanding its opera-
tions; it has so many different movements,
and these succeed each other so rapidly, that
its ways become indiscernible.

God, whose knowledge is infinite, can alone
read clearly into its recesses, and fathom its
most secret foldings. He sees our thoughts,
even before we have formed them; he discovers our most hidden paths, he views all our
stratagems and evasions. This is what occa-

sioned the royal prophet to say, "Thy knowledge has become wonderful to me; it is high, and I can not reach to it" (Ps. 138:6). To reflect on all our ordinary actions by a continual self-examination would be to entangle ourselves in a labyrinth from which we could never be extricated. Besides this, the continual attention and restraint would be insupportable if it were necessary by incessant reflection to enter into ourselves and to remember that we are thinking, to observe that we are considering, to see that we are seeing, to discern that we are discerning, to reflect that we are meditating. In this confusion and variety of thoughts the mind would engage itself in a labyrinth from whose mazes it would vainly seek to disengage itself. We may infer from this, that only persons endowed with the spirit of prayer can clearly explain this subject. Moreover, by prayer we do not here understand it in the sense of St. Basil, who confounds it with the simple petitions which the faithful offer to God when they implore any grace from his clemency; but according to the definition of St. Bonaventura, who says that prayer, in general, comprehends all the acts of contemplation; or in the sense of St. Gregory of Nyssa, who calls it a conversation between the soul and God; or of St. Chrysostom, who speaks of it as an interview with the Divine Majesty; or, in fine, of St. Augustine and St. John of Damascus, who calls it an elevation of the soul to God—a transport of the mind in God. But if it be an elevation of the soul, an interview, a conversation, it is certain that by prayer we converse with God, and that in return the Almighty speaks to us; that we tend to God, and that God descends to us; that we live— that we breathe in God, and that reciprocally, the Almighty dwells in us, and infuses his spirit into our souls.

But what is the subject of our interview in prayer? It is God. For what can a person inflamed with love speak of, but the object of his affections. On this account, prayer and mystical theology are but one and the same thing. It is called theology, because it has God for its object, as well as the speculative theology taught in schools; but there are three points in which a difference exists. First, scholastic theology treats of the Almighty as God, and considers the Divinity in the Supreme Goodness; mystical theology treats of the Almighty as a being sovereignly amiable, and considers the supreme goodness in the Divinity. Second, speculative theology speaks of God to man and with man; mystical theology treats of God to God, and with God himself. Third, the end of speculative theol-

ogy is to teach us to know God; and the object
of mystical theology is to teach us to love him.
One produces learned men, doctors, theologians; whilst the other forms saints, ardent
lovers of the Almighty, devoted to his service
and burning with zeal for his interests.

This theology is called mystical, because it
is concealed. The conversation which passes
in prayer between God and the soul is carried
on in the secret recesses of the heart; it is a
communication of feelings impenetrable to all
but those who speak. The language of friends
is of so singular a nature that it can be understood only by themselves. "I sleep and my
heart watcheth," said the sacred Lover, "the
voice of my beloved knocking" (Song of Songs
5:2). Who would have imagined that this
holy Spouse conversed with her Beloved even
when asleep? Yet it was the case; because
where love reigns, the sound of words and the
ministry of the senses are unnecessary for the
conveyance of sentiments and ideas. Prayer,
or mystical theology, is, then, nothing more
than an amorous intercourse between the soul
and God; the subject of this interview is the
sovereign and infinitely amiable goodness, to
which the soul longs to be united.

Prayer may be called a manna, on account
of the different flavors and divine sweets
which love discovers to those who make use of

it. But it is a hidden manna which falls in the desert before the dawn of day; that is to say, it is not the fruit of lights and science; its sweets can be tasted only in solitude. When we converse with God alone, then we may say of the soul, "Who is she that goeth up by the desert, as a pillar of smoke of aromatical spices, of myrrh and frankincense, and of all the powders of the perfumer?" (Song of Songs 3:6). It is the Spouse herself, who intreats her Beloved to conduct her into solitude, that they may both converse in secret: "Come, my Beloved, let us go forth into the field: let us abide in the villages" (Song of Songs 7:11). On this account the sacred Lover is compared to the turtle dove, which seeks gloomy and lonely spots, and there warbles her melody to gratify her mate during his life and to mourn for him when dead.

It is also for this reason that the holy Spouse and her divine Lover represent their reciprocal love under the idea of a continual interview. If their friends sometimes mingle in the conversation, it is without interrupting or disturbing it, for a short time only, as it were, by stealth. The great attraction which persons of prayer experience is to converse with God in perfect solitude. The blessed mother Theresa of Jesus relates of herself, that in the commencement of her spiritual career she had a singular devotion to those mysteries which represent only the person of our Lord; as during his prayer in the Garden of Olives, or when he waited for the Samaritan woman near the well; she thought, that when her divine Master was alone he would attract her more powerfully, and that she should be sooner united to him.

Love seeks not for witnesses of its words; and even when those who love have nothing to communicate which requires secrecy, they take pleasure in conversing in private. The reason of this probably is, that they speak only for each other; and it would seem to them they did not speak for themselves alone if their interview could be overheard. Besides this, they make the most ordinary observations in a manner so peculiar as to mark the love from which their words proceed. There is nothing uncommon in the words they use; but the tone, the emphasis, and the manner which accompanies every thing they say render their language so singular that they alone can understand it. The title of friend publicly conferred on any individual signifies but little; but when uttered in private it comprehends a great deal, and becomes more expressive in proportion to the secrecy with which it is spoken.

If we compare several theologians who speak

eloquently of the Almighty, but who love him little, with those who loved him ardently, as the Ignatiuses, the Cyprians, the Chrysostoms, the Augustines, the Hilaries, the Ephrems, the Gregories, the Bernards, and several other illustrious men of antiquity, oh! what a difference shall we discover in their language! We all use the same expressions; but the words pronounced by those lovers of the Almighty were inflamed and embalmed, if we may say so, with the delicious perfume of divine love; whereas, with us they are only cold expressions, which contain neither the energy nor the sweetness of charity.

Everything speaks in those who love: not only their tongue, but also their eyes; their sighs, their countenance, their very silence is eloquent. "My heart hath said to thee: My face hath sought thee: thy face, O Lord, will I still seek" (Ps. 26: 8). "My eyes have failed for thy word, saying, When wilt thou comfort me?" (Ps. 118: 82). "Hear, O Lord, my prayer: give ear to my supplication in thy truth" (Ps. 142: 1). "Give thyself no rest, and let not the apple of thy eye cease," said the inhabitants of Jerusalem, addressing their desolate city (Lam. 2:18). Those who love, need not speak to express their affliction: they can make themselves understood by the motion of their eyes and the abundance of their tears.

As the principal exercise of mystical theology is speaking to God and listening to his voice, which is heard in the hidden recesses of the heart, and as this conversation is carried on in secret, commenced and continued without the help of words, by aspirations on the part of the soul and inspirations on the part of God, may we not justly call it a prayer of silence, in which the eyes speak to the eyes, and the heart to the heart, and in which no one can hear what passes except God and the soul, who converse together?

Of the Union of the Soul With God In Prayer

Of the Manner In Which Love Unites the Soul With God In Prayer

We do not allude at present to the general union of the heart with God common to all who possess the habit of charity, but to certain particular acts produced by prayer, whereby the soul already united to God inclines to a still more intimate union with his sovereign goodness. There is a great difference between simply uniting two things, and pressing them closely together. To join two objects nothing more is necessary than a simple application, which unites without leaving any interval between them. The vine is united in this manner to the elm tree, and thus also the jasmine twines round arbors which may be seen in gardens. But to press two things is to unite them closely, and this can only be effected by a strong application, which increases the power of union. Ivy is joined in this manner to trees; it is not only united, but so closely bound thereto as to penetrate their bark.

Francis of Sales

The comparison furnished by the love of infants for their mothers should not be forgotten, had we no other motive for pursuing it than the idea of innocence it conveys to the mind. We see a mother quietly seated near her beloved nursling, who on its side, endeavors to throw itself into her arms, and compress its body within the limits of its mother's bosom. She embraces her dear child, and presses it to her heart, whilst the infant attracted by her caresses, contributes to increase the union with its mother by its little exertions, which seem to express its desire to return again to the womb, from which it has but just sprung to life.

Union is then perfect, because tho in itself one and simple, it proceeds from two persons who both contribute thereto, yet in such a manner that it depends entirely on the mother. Beside, being the first to attract the child, she is also the first to receive it in her arms and press it to her heart, the infant not having power to unite itself so intimately to its parent. Yet it exerts all its strength; it permits itself to be attracted, and even contributes to union as far as its little efforts allow—those efforts, indeed, are so feeble, that they are mere attempts at forming a union.

Thus, the Almighty, discovering to the devout soul the fathomless abyss of his love,

draws her to him, and after having united and
concentrated all her powers in himself, causes
her sweetly to repose on the bosom of his more
than maternal tenderness; he embraces and
presses her closely in the arms of his mercy,
with the lips of his infinite goodness he gives
her "the kiss of his mouth," and uniting her
to the bosom of his love, convinces her by experience, that the breasts of her divine Spouse
are better than wine (Song of Songs 1:1).
The soul, allured by the heavenly sweetness of
these caresses, not only consents to the means
the Almighty employs for uniting her to him,
but exerts her utmost endeavors to attach herself intimately to his sovereign goodness. But
notwithstanding all her efforts, she feels and
acknowledges that she owes her union with
God to the operation of God himself, without
which she could not make the least advance-
ment toward his divine Majesty.

We say of a person, who looks earnestly at
a great beauty, that his eyes are riveted on
her countenance; that a fine piece of music, to
which we listen with extraordinary attention
captivates the ears; that an eloquent discourse
chains the hearts of the auditors when they
listen to it with great earnestness. By fas-
cinating the eyes, captivating the ears, and
ravishing the heart is meant closely applying
and uniting these senses and powers to the

objects which occupy them. We may say, that the soul is closely united to its object, when it loves and devotes a great deal of its attention thereto. The term "to press," in this sense, only means to augment, to strengthen, and to perfect union. Custom has rendered this expression familiar in conversation. We say, he presses me to do such a thing, he presses me to stay; that is, he not only employs persuasion and entreaties to induce me to accede to his wishes, but he does so at all times, and to the full extent of his power. Thus, the pilgrims of Emmaus prest Jesus Christ to such a degree as to employ a kind of gentle violence, to constrain him to remain with them.

In prayer, union is often effected by short but frequent aspirations of the soul to God. As infants at the breast endeavor from time to time to press themselves more closely to their mother's bosom, so a soul united to God in prayer endeavors to unite itself more intimately, and to penetrate more deeply into the divine delights it enjoys. For example, a soul which has long and tranquilly felt the happiness of belonging to God by union will suddenly make an effort to increase this happiness by cementing her union still more closely. She will say to him, I am thine, wholly thine, O Lord, and I desire to belong to thee more perfectly and unreservedly. Attract me, O divine Jesus! into the innermost recess of thy adorable heart, that I may be totally absorbed and engulfed in thy infinite love and sovereign amiability.

Union is produced at other times not by reiterated transports but by a constant and imperceptible movement of the heart, which penetrates more deeply into the abyss of the divine goodness in proportion as it becomes more intimately united thereto. We need not lean on a heavy mass of stone, lead, or metal, to make it press the earth on which it is laid; its own weight, which always inclines it toward its center, is sufficient to sink it so far into the earth that in time it becomes buried beneath its surface.

Thus, when our heart is perseveringly and uninterruptedly united to God, it ceases not to advance, by an insensible progression, until it becomes totally absorbed in God. This proceeds from the inclination produced by divine love, which inclines it to an ever-increasing union with the sovereign goodness. (As the great apostle of France has observed, Love is a unitive virtue, that is, a virtue which disposes to union with the sovereign good.) During our exile here below, divine love is a continual movement, or at least an active habit, tending to motion; therefore, even when love has attained to union, it continues still to act imperceptibly, in order to increase and perfect the union, which has been commenced.

Trees which have been transplanted, shoot new roots, and extend far into the bosom of the earth, which is their element and nourishment; but we are not aware of this progress during its continuation, it is perceptible only when completely effected. So it is with the human heart after it has been transplanted, as it were, into the bosom of God, by divine love, if it make prayer its constant occupation, it is continually dilated, and incessantly penetrates more deeply into the abyss of the sovereign goodness to be more inseparably united thereto. But the progress of this union is imperceptible, and can be observed only when complete.

In drinking a strong liquid you united it to yourself by swallowing and receiving it into your stomach; for in this sense simple union and the act of receiving are but one and the same thing. This union, increasing by almost imperceptible degrees, which gradually become sensible, is soon very powerful and active. You perceive that the virtue of this liquid insinuates itself into every part of your frame—that it fortifies the head, exhilarates the heart, and gives strength and activity to the vital spirits.

Thus, a single sentiment of love—for example, a conviction of God's goodness, when it enters the heart—is sufficient to produce union with God; but if this feeling be entertained for any time, it becomes like a precious perfume, which penetrates every faculty of the soul, and which in evaporating diffuses itself in the will and is incorporated with the mind.

To exemplify this truth, the psalmist compares the word of God to honey, whose sweetness is more perfectly felt by the palate when it is retained for a long time in the mouth. We may reason in the same manner on a feeling of love for the sovereign goodness of God. It may be exprest by these words of St. Bruno: "O Goodness!"—by the aspiration of St. Thomas, "My Lord and my God!"—by that of St. Mary Magdalene, "Master!"—or, in fine, by that of St. Francis, "My God and my all!" This feeling, provided it be entertained for some time in a heart inflamed with love, will not fail to extend its influence and to penetrate very deeply; that is, it will increase and perfect union, so that the soul, being thoroughly imbued with this sentiment, will scarcely be distinguishable from it.

Something similar occurs when balm or any perfume is drop on cotton; they become so united and incorporated, that it is difficult to discern whether it be perfume or only perfumed cotton.

Happy the soul which, inflamed with love, carefully preserves, amidst the unruffled calm and peace of her heart, the sacred feeling and conviction of the presence of God! By this means, her union with the divine goodness will always increase, tho by imperceptible degrees, and she will in the end find herself penetrated and imbued, if I may venture to use the expression, with the infinite sweetness of God. In the feeling of the presence of God, to which I here allude, there is nothing sensible in which the inferior part of the soul might have a share; it resides in the superior part, which we have called the most elevated region of the soul, in which is placed the throne of divine love, whereon it performs its most sublime and exalted functions.

Love Is the Life of the Soul

The soul is the first cause of all the vital movements or actions of man, and as Aristotle says, it is the principle by which we live, feel, and hear. Whence it follows that the movements produced by the soul are the only criterion for judging of the kind of life by which we are animated, and that where there is no natural motion there can be no life. This being established, it is evident that the love which animates our soul is the principle of our spiritual life by which we live, feel, and move, conformably to this life. It is also clear that our spiritual life is of the same nature as our affections; that a heart which has no motion, that has no affection, must be destitute of love; whereas it can not be deprived of motion when animated by charity.

We can not make Jesus Christ the object of our love without placing in him our spiritual life, and as he is concealed in God in heaven, as the divinity was hidden in Jesus Christ on earth, St. Paul was right in his conclusion, that our life is now hidden in Jesus Christ, and that when Christ our life and our love shall appear, we shall also appear with him in God.

The holy martyr, St. Ignatius, exprest his conviction of this truth, by saying, "my love is crucified." The natural and carnal love, which was the principle of my mortal life, has been immolated on the cross with all the passions of which it is the source; it has died because it was mortal. But as my Savior gave up his mortal existence on the cross only to exchange it for an immortal life, so in dying spiritually with him, I have only sacrificed a natural love, which was the source of a life subject to the law of death, to receive in exchange a heavenly, and consequently an immortal love, which has been to me the commencement of a supernatural existence.

We have an infallible rule for discerning a real from a false ecstasy. A soul may be transported beyond herself in prayer; but if she be not habitually united to God and elevated to the divinity by a life superior to nature and the senses, if her conduct do not visibly display that ecstasy of action and operation which is accomplished by a renunciation of worldly desires, of self-will, of the inclinations of corrupt nature, and the practise of interior virtues, as humility of heart, meekness, simplicity, a constant tender charity for our neighbor, her prayer should be distrusted; her raptures serve only to attract the admiration of men without rendering her more pleasing in the sight of God.

What does it avail a soul to be transported above her sphere in prayer, if her life, which is a succession of terrestrial affections, of base and natural actions, be only another ecstasy, which degrades the dignity of her nature? To be elevated in prayer not only above self but even as high as the very angels, and by our actions to rank ourselves with beasts, is to resemble the persons mentioned in the sacred text, who "halt between two sides" (1 Kings 18:21); or those, who having sworn "by the

Lord, swear by Melchom'' (Zeph. 1:5).
Should not raptures be considered deceits and
illusions of the devil, when our conduct is so
directly opposed to them?

Happy those who desire no other elevation
than to lead a supernatural and consequently
an ecstatic life! Such persons should not grieve
at not being favored with the raptures which
accompany the prayers of others. There are
many blessed souls in heaven who never had
raptures of contemplation on earth. In read-
ing the history of all the servants of God, we
shall see numerous martyrs and eminent saints
of both sexes on whom the Almighty bestowed
no other favor in prayer than the grace of
devotion and fervor. But we shall find that
by overcoming themselves, and conquering
their natural inclinations, they all passed their
lives in the ecstasy of action or operation.

Is it not evident that this is the ecstasy St.
Paul had principally in view, when he said,
''I live, now not I, but Christ liveth in me''
(Gal. 2:20). He explains himself still more
clearly, in his epistle to the Romans, when he
says, ''our old man is crucified with him, that
the body of sin may be destroyed, and that we
may serve sin no longer. That as Christ is
risen from the dead by the glory of the Father,
so we also may walk in newness of life''
(Rom. 6:6, 4).

There are then in each of us, as it were, two separate persons, consequently two distinct lives; an old man with an old life, and a new man with a new life. These two lives are incompatible, and in this point we may be compared to the eagle, which can not remain long on the wing when it becomes old, because its strength is exhausted; but after having shed its old feathers, which it shakes into the sea, it gets new ones, accompanied with renewed vigor and youth.

Thus, our first life, which is that of the old man, retains the faults, the weaknesses, and infirmities contracted by original sin. We then live to the sin of Adam, with a life subject to death, which in the language of St. Paul is death itself. In the second species of existence, which is according to the new man, that is, a life conformable to grace, and to the benefits, the precepts, and the adorable will of our divine Savior, we live not to sin, but to salvation and redemption; everything regarding this life may be called vital and vivifying.

To attain this life, we must walk through the path of death, that is, we must crucify our flesh, with its passions and inordinate desires; we must be plunged in the waters of baptism and penance; we must follow the example of Naaman, who drowned his leprosy in the Jordan, from which he came out purified and healed. After his cure he might be said to be no longer the old Naaman, whom the corruption and infection of his body rendered insupportable; he might be called a new Naaman, purified and healed, because he had died to his leprosy, to commence a new life consisting in corporal health and vigor.

It follows from what has been said that a soul, which by the grace of Jesus Christ has risen to a new life, no longer lives for herself, in herself, or to herself, but in her Savior, to her Savior, and solely for her Savior. This is the conclusion drawn by St. Paul when he says, "Reckon yourselves to be dead indeed to sin, but alive to God in Christ Jesus our Lord" (Rom. 6:11).

The Devout Life

What True Devotion Is

You aim at a devout life, beloved, because as a Christian you know that such devotion is most acceptable to God's divine majesty. But seeing that the small errors people are wont to commit in the beginning of any undertaking are apt to wax greater as they advance, and to become irreparable at last, it is most important that you should thoroughly understand wherein lies the grace of true devotion; and that because while there undoubtedly is such a true devotion, there are also many spurious and idle semblances thereof; and unless you know which is real, you may mistake, and waste your energy in pursuing an empty, profitless shadow. Arellius was wont to paint all his pictures with the features and expression of the women he loved, and even so we all color devotion according to our own likings and dispositions. One man sets great value on fasting, and believes himself to be leading a very devout life so long as he fasts rigorously, altho the while his heart is full of bitterness; and while he will not moisten his lips with wine, perhaps not even with water, in his great abstinence, he does not scruple to steep them in his neighbor's blood, through slander and detraction. Another man reckons himself as devout because he repeats many prayers daily, altho at the same time he does not refrain from all manner of angry, irritating, conceited, or insulting speeches among his family and neighbors. This man freely opens his purse in almsgiving, but closes his heart to all gentle and forgiving feelings toward those who are opposed to him; while that one is ready enough to forgive his enemies, but will never pay his rightful debts save under pressure. Meanwhile all these people are conventionally called religious, but nevertheless they are in no true sense really devout. When Saul's servants sought to take David, Michael induced them to suppose that the lifeless figure lying in his bed, and covered with his garments, was the man they sought; and in like manner many people dress up an exterior with the visible acts expressive of earnest devotion, and the world supposes them to be really devout and spiritually minded, while all the time they are mere "lay" figures, mere phantasms of devotion.

But, in fact, all true and living devotion presupposes the love of God; and indeed it is neither more nor less than a very real love of

God, tho not always of the same kind; for that love, one while shining on the soul, we call grace, which makes us acceptable to his divine majesty; when it strengthens us to do well, it is called charity; but when it attains its fullest perfection, in which it not only leads us to do well, but to act carefully, diligently, and promptly, then it is called devotion. The ostrich never flies, the hen rises with difficulty, and achieves but a brief and rare flight, but the eagle, the dove, and the swallow, are continually on the wing, and soar high; even so sinners do not rise toward God, for all their movements are earthly and earth-bound. Well-meaning people, who have not as yet attained a true devotion, attempt a manner of flight by means of their good actions, but rarely, slowly, and heavily; while really devout men rise up to God frequently, and with a swift and soaring wing. In short, devotion is simply a spiritual activity and liveliness by means of which divine love works in us, and causes us to work briskly and lovingly; and just as charity leads us to a general practise of all God's commandments, so devotion leads us to practise them readily and diligently. And therefore we can not call him who neglects to observe all God's commandments either good or devout, because in order to be good, a man must be filled with love, and to be devout, he must further be very ready and apt to perform the deeds of love. And forasmuch as devotion consists in a high degree of real love, it not only makes us ready, active, and diligent in following all God's commands, but it also excites us to be ready and loving in performing as many good works as possible, even such as are not enjoined upon us, but are only matters of counsel or inspiration. Even as a man just recovering from illness, walks only so far as he is obliged to go, with a slow and weary step, so the converted sinner journeys along as far as God commands him, but slowly and wearily, until he attains a true spirit of devotion, and then, like a sound man, he not only gets along, but he runs and leaps in the way of God's commandments, and hastens gladly along the paths of heavenly counsels and inspirations. The difference between love and devotion is just that which exists between fire and flame; love being a spiritual fire which becomes devotion when it is fanned into a flame; and what devotion adds to the fire of love is that flame which makes it eager, energetic and diligent, not merely in obeying God's commandments, but in fulfilling his divine counsels and inspirations.

The Nature and Excellence of Devotion

Those who sought to discourage the Israelites from going up to the promised land, told
them that it was "a land which eateth up the
inhabitants thereof" (Num. 13:32); that is,
that the climate was so unhealthy that the
inhabitants could not live long, and that the
people thereof were "men of a great stature,"
who looked upon the newcomers as mere
locusts to be devoured. It is just so, beloved,
that the world runs down true devotion, paint-
ing devout people with gloomy, melancholy
aspect, and affirming that religion makes them
dismal and unpleasant. But even as Joshua
and Caleb protested that not only was the
promised land a fair and pleasant country,
but that the Israelites would take an easy and
peaceful possession thereof; so the Holy Spirit
tells us through his saints, and our Lord has
told us with his own lips, that a devout life is
very sweet, very happy, and very lovable.

The world, looking on, sees that devout persons fast, watch and pray, endure injury
patiently, minister to the sick and poor, restrain their temper, check and subdue their
passions, deny themselves in all sensual indul-
gence, and do many other things which in
themselves are hard and difficult. But the

world sees nothing of that inward, heartfelt devotion which makes all these actions pleasant and easy. Watch a bee hovering over the mountain thyme; the juices it gathers are bitter, but the bee turns them all to honey, and so tells the worldling that tho the devout soul finds bitter herbs along its path of devotion, they are all turned to sweetness and pleasantness as it treads; and the martyrs have counted fire, sword, and rack but as perfumed flowers by reason of their devotion. And if devotion can sweeten such cruel torments, and even death itself, how much more will it give a charm to ordinary good deeds? We sweeten unripe fruit with sugar, and it is useful in correcting the crudity even of that which is good. So devotion is the real spiritual sweetness which takes away all bitterness from mortifications; and prevents consolations from disagreeing with the soul; it cures the poor of sadness and the rich of presumption; it keeps the opprest from feeling desolate and the prosperous from insolence; it averts sadness from the lonely and dissipation from social life; it is as warmth in winter and refreshing dew in summer; it knows how to abound and how to suffer want, how to profit alike by honor and contempt; it accepts gladness and sadness with an even mind, and fills men's hearts with a wondrous sweetness.

Ponder upon Jacob's ladder: it is a true
picture of the devout life; the two poles which
support the steps are types of prayer which
seeks the love of God, and the sacraments
which confer that love; while the steps themselves are simply the degrees of love by which
we go on from virtue to virtue, either descend-
ing by good deeds on behalf of our neighbor
or ascending by contemplation to a loving
union with God. Consider, too, who they are
who trod this ladder; men with angels' hearts,
or angels with human forms. They are not
youthful, but they seem to be so by reason of
their vigor and spiritual activity. They have
wings wherewith to fly, and attain to God in
holy prayer, but they have likewise feet wherewith to tread in human paths by a holy
gracious intercourse with men; their faces are
bright and beautiful, inasmuch as they accept
all things gently and sweetly; their heads and
limbs are uncovered, because their thoughts,
affections and actions have no motive or object
save that of pleasing God; the rest of their
bodies is covered with a light shining garment,
because while they use the world and the
things of this life, they use all such purely
and honestly, and no further than is needful
for their condition. Such are the truly devout.
Believe me, dearly beloved, devotion is the
sweetest of sweets, the queen of virtues, the

perfection of love. If love is the milk of life, devotion is the cream thereof; if it is a fruitful plant, devotion is the blossom; if it is a precious stone, devotion is its brightness; if it is a precious balm, devotion is its perfume, even that sweet odor which delights men and causes the angels to rejoice.

Devotion Is Suitable to Every Vocation and Profession

When God created the world he commanded each tree to bear fruit after its kind; and even so he bids Christians, the living trees of his Church, to bring forth fruits of devotion, each one according to his kind and vocation. A different exercise of devotion is required of each, the noble, the artizan, the servant, the prince, the maiden, and the wife; and furthermore such practise must be modified according to the strength, the calling, and the duties of each individual. . . . And if the father of a family were as regardless in making provision for the future as a Capucin, if the artizan spent the day in church like a religious, . . . would not such a devotion be ridiculous, ill-regulated, and intolerable? Nevertheless, such a mistake is often made, and the world, which can not or will not discriminate between

real devotion and the indiscretion of those who
fancy themselves devout, grumbles and finds
fault with devotion, which is really nowise
concerned in these errors. No, indeed, my
friend, the devotion which is true hinders
nothing, but on the contrary it perfects everything; and that which runs counter to the
rightful vocation of any one is, you may be
sure, a spurious devotion. Aristotle says that
the bee sucks honey from flowers without
damaging them, leaving them as whole and
fresh as it found them; but true devotion does
better still, for it not only hinders no manner
of vocation or duty, but, contrariwise, it
adorns and beautifies all. Throw precious
stones into honey, and each will grow more
brilliant according to its several color; and
in like manner everybody fulfils his special
calling better when subject to the influence of
devotion: family duties are lighter, married
love truer, service to our King more faithful,
every kind of occupation more acceptable and
better performed where that is the guide.

It is an error, nay more, a very heresy, to
seek to banish the devout life from the soldier's
guardroom, the mechanic's workshop, the
prince's court, or the domestic hearth. Of
course a purely contemplative devotion, such
as is specially proper to the religious and
monastic life, can not be practised in these

outer vocations, but there are various other kinds of devotion well-suited to lead those whose calling is secular, along the paths of perfection. The Old Testament furnishes us with examples in Abraham, Isaac and Jacob, David, Job, Tobias, Sarah, Rebecca, and Judith; and in the New Testament we read of St. Joseph, Lydia and Crispus, who led a perfectly devout life in their trades: we have St. Anne, Martha, St. Monica, Aquila and Priscilla, as examples of household devotion; Cornelius, St. Sebastian, and St. Maurice among soldiers; Constantine, St. Helena, St. Louis, the Blessed, Amadæus, and St. Edward on the throne. And we even find instances of some who fell away in solitude, usually so helpful to perfection, some who had led a higher life in the world, which seems so antagonistic to it. St. Gregory dwells on how Lot, who had kept himself pure in the city, fell in his mountain solitude. Be sure that wheresoever our lot is cast we may and must aim at the perfect life.

The First Step Must Be the Purifying of the Soul

"The flowers appear on the earth" (Song of Songs 2:12), says the heavenly Bridegroom, and the time for pruning and cutting is come.

And what, my child, are our hearts' flowers save our good desires? Now, so soon as these begin to appear, we need the pruning-hook to cut off all dead and superfluous works from our conscience. When the daughter of a strange land was about to espouse an Israelite, the law commanded her to put off the garment of her captivity, to pare her nails, and to shave her head (Deut. 21:12); even so the soul which aims at the dignity of becoming the spouse of Christ must put off the old man, and put on the new man, forsaking sin; moreover, it must pare and shave away every impediment which can hinder the love of God. The very first step toward spiritual health is to be purged from our sinful humors. St. Paul received perfect purification instantaneously, and the like grace was conferred on St. M. Magdalene, St. Catherine of Genoa, St. Pelagia, and some others, but this kind of purgation is as miraculous and extraordinary in grace as the resurrection of the dead in nature, nor dare we venture to aspire to it. The ordinary purification, whether of body or soul, is accomplished only by slow degrees, step by step, gradually and painfully.

The angels on Jacob's ladder had wings, yet nevertheless they did not fly, but went in due order up and down the steps of the ladder. The soul which rises from out of sin to a devout life has been compared to the dawn, which does not banish darkness suddenly, but by degrees. That cure which is gradually effected is always the surest; and spiritual maladies, like those of the body, are wont to come on horseback and express, while they depart slowly and on foot. So that we must needs be brave and patient, beloved, in this undertaking. It is a woful thing to see souls beginning to chafe and grow disheartened because they find themselves still subject to imperfection after having made some attempt at leading a devout life, and well nigh yielding to the temptation to give up in despair and fall back; but, on the other hand, there is an extreme danger surrounding those souls who, through the opposite temptation, are disposed to imagine themselves purified from all imperfection at the very outset of their purgation; who count themselves as full-grown almost before they are born, and seek to fly before they have wings. Be sure, daughter, that these are in great danger of a relapse through having left their physician too soon. "It is but lost labor to rise up early and late take rest," unless the Lord prosper all we do.

The work of the soul's purification neither may nor can end save with life itself; do not then let us be disheartened by our imperfections, our very perfection lies in diligently

contending against them, and it is impossible
so to contend without seeing them, or to overcome without meeting them face to face. Our
victory does not consist in being insensible to
them, but in not consenting to them. Now to
be afflicted by our imperfections is certainly
not to consent thereto, and for the furtherance
of humility it is needful that we sometimes
find ourselves worsted in this spiritual battle,
wherein, however, we shall never be conquered
until we lose either life or courage. Moreover, imperfections and venial sins can not
destroy our spiritual life, which is only to be
lost through deadly sin; consequently we have
only need to watch well that they do not im-
peril our courage. David continually asks the
Lord to strengthen his heart against cowardice
and discouragement; and it is our privilege
in this war that we are certain to vanquish
so long as we are willing to fight.

The First Purification, Namely, From Deadly Sin

The first purification to be made is from
sin; the means whereby to make it, is true
repentance. Use one of the many little books
written in order to help your examination of
conscience. Read some such book carefully,

examining point by point wherein you have sinned, from the first use of your reason to the present time. And if you mistrust your memory, write down the result of your examination. Having thus sought out the evil spots in your conscience, strive to detest them, and to reject them with the greatest abhorrence and contrition of which your heart is capable; bearing in mind these four things: that by sin you have lost God's grace, rejected your portion in heaven, incurred the pains of hell, and renounced God's eternal love. You see, beloved, that I am now speaking of a general confession of the sins of your whole life, which appertains to true repentance, and will be found most helpful in the beginning of your pursuit after holiness, and therefore I earnestly advise you to make it. Persons leading an every-day life not unfrequently fail in confessing their sins, because they do not prepare sufficiently carefully, and have not the needful contrition. Owing to this deficiency such people confess their sins with a tacit intention of returning to their old sins, inasmuch as they will not avoid the occasions of sin or take the necessary measures for amendment of life, and so a confession which goes to the root of their sins is required to steady and fix the soul. But furthermore such a confession forces us to a clearer self-knowledge, kindles a wholesome shame for our past life, and rouses gratitude for God's mercy, which has so long waited patiently for us, it comforts the heart, refreshes the spirit, excites good resolutions, affords opportunity to God's minister if we open our griefs to him for giving the most suitable advice, and disposes us to confess our sins more effectually for the future, therefore I can not enter into the subject of a general change of life, and entire turning to God, by means of a devout life, without urging upon you the absolute necessity that your repentance should be deep and true.

Of Creation

CONSIDERATIONS: 1. Consider that but a few years since you were not born into the world, and your soul had as yet no existence. Where wert thou then, O my soul? the world was already old, and yet of thee there was no sign.

2. God brought you out of this nothingness, in order to make you what you are, not because he had any need of you, but solely out of his goodness.

3. Consider the being which God has given you; for it is the highest being of this visible world, adapted to live eternally, and to be perfectly united to God's divine majesty.

AFFECTIONS AND RESOLUTIONS: **1.** Humble yourself utterly before God, saying with the psalmist, O Lord, I am nothing in respect of thee; what am I, that thou shouldst remember me? O my soul, thou wert yet lost in that abyss of nothingness, if God had not called thee forth, and what of thee in such a case?

2. Give God thanks. O great and good Creator, what do I not owe thee, who didst take me from out that nothingness, by thy mercy to make me what I am? How can I ever do enough worthily to praise thy holy name and render due thanks to thy goodness?

3. Confess your own shame. But alas, O my Creator, so far from uniting myself to thee by a loving service, I have rebelled against thee through my unruly affections, departing from thee, and giving myself up to sin, and ignoring thy goodness, as tho thou hadst not created me.

4. Prostrate thyself before God. O my soul, know that the Lord he is thy God, it is he that hath made thee, and not thou thyself. O God, I am the work of thy hands; henceforth I will not seek to rest in myself, who am naught. Wherein hast thou to glory, who art but dust and ashes? how canst thou, a very nothing, exalt thyself? In order to my own humiliation, I will do such and such a thing, I will endure such contempt: I will alter my ways and henceforth follow my Creator, and realize that I am honored by his calling me to the being he has given me; I will employ it solely to obey his will, by means of the teaching which he gives me in his Church and through his ministers.

CONCLUSION: 1. Thank God. Bless the Lord, O my soul, and praise his holy name with all thy being, because his goodness called me forth from nothingness, and his mercy created me.

2. Offer yourself. O my God, I offer thee with all my heart the being thou hast given me, I dedicate and consecrate it to thee.

3. Pray. O God, strengthen me in these affections and resolutions. Dear Lord, I commend myself, and all those I love, to thy never-failing mercy.

Our Father, etc.

4. At the end of your meditation linger a while, and gather, so to say, a little spiritual bouquet from the thoughts you have dwelt upon, the sweet perfume whereof may refresh you through the day.

How to Practise True Repentance

Such meditations . . . beloved, will help you, and having made them, go on bravely in the spirit of humility to practise true repentance; and I entreat you, be not troubled by any sort of fearfulness. The scorpion who stings us is venomous, but when his oil has been distilled, it is the best remedy for his bite; even so sin is shameful when we commit it, but when it is truly repented of, it loses its bitterness. Contrition, confession of sin, and amendment of life are, through God's mercy, so sweet-savored, that the ugliness of sin is effaced, and its ill-savor dispersed by the practise of them. Simon the leper called the Magdalen a sinner (Mark 14; Luke 7 : 38), but our Lord turned the discourse to the perfume of her ointment and the greatness of her love. If we are really humble, beloved, our sins will be infinitely displeasing to us, because they offend God; but it will be welcome and sweet to accuse ourselves thereof, because in so doing we honor God; and there is always somewhat soothing in fully telling the physician all details of our pain.

It Is Needful to Put Away All Inclination for Useless and Dangerous Things

Sports, balls, plays, festivities, pomps, are not in themselves evil, but rather indifferent matters, capable of being used for good or ill; but nevertheless they are dangerous, and it is

Francis of Sales

still more dangerous to take great delight in
them. Therefore, my friend, I say that altho
it is lawful to amuse yourself, to dance, dress,
feast, and see seemly plays, at the same time,
if you are much addicted to these things, they
will hinder your devotion, and become ex-
tremely hurtful and dangerous to you. The
harm lies, not in doing them, but in the degree to which you care for them. It is a
pity to sow the seed of vain and foolish tastes
in the soil of your heart, taking up the place
of better things, and hindering the soul from
cultivating good dispositions. It was thus that
the Nazarites of old abstained not merely from
all intoxicating liquors, but from grapes fresh
or dried, and from vinegar, not because these
were intoxicating, but because they might
excite the desire for fermented liquors. Just
so, while I do not forbid the use of these
dangerous pleasures, I say that you can not
take an excessive delight in them without their
telling upon your devotion. When the stag
has waxed fat he hides himself amid the
thicket, conscious that his fleetness is impaired
should he be in need to fly: and so the human
heart which is cumbered with useless, superfluous, dangerous attachments, becomes in-
capacitated for that earnest following after
God which is the true life of devotion. No
one blames children for running after butter-

143

flies, because they are children; but is it not ridiculous and pitiful to see full-grown men eager about such worthless trifles as the worldly amusements before named, which are likely to throw them off their balance and disturb their spiritual life? Therefore, dear friend, I would have you cleanse your heart from all such tastes, remembering that while the acts themselves are not necessarily incompatible with a devout life, all delight in them must be harmful.

All Evil Inclinations Must Be Purged Away

Furthermore, beloved, we have certain natural inclinations, which are not strictly speaking either deadly or venial sins, but rather imperfections; and the acts in which they take shape, failings and deficiencies. Thus St. Jerome says that St. Paula had so strong a tendency to excessive sorrow that when she lost her husband and children she nearly died of grief: that was not a sin, but an imperfection, since it did not depend upon her wish and will. Some people are naturally easy, some the opposite; some are indisposed to accept other men's opinions, some naturally disposed to be cross, some to be affectionate; in short, there is hardly any one in whom

some such imperfections do not exist. Now,
altho they be natural and instinctive in each
person, they may be remedied and corrected,
or even eradicated, by cultivating the reverse disposition. And this, beloved, must be
done. Gardeners have found how to make the
bitter almond-tree bear sweet fruit by graft-
ing the juice of the latter upon it, why should
we not purge out our perverse dispositions
and infuse such as are good? There is no
disposition so good but it may be made bad
by dint of vicious habits, and neither is there
any natural disposition so perverse but that
it may be conquered and overcome by God's
grace primarily, and then by our earnest, diligent endeavor. . . .

Gentleness Toward Others and Reme-
dies Against Anger

The holy chrism, used by the Church according to apostolic tradition, was made of
olive oil mingled with balm, which, among
other things, are emblematic of two virtues
very specially conspicuous in our dear Lord
himself, which he has specially commended
to us, as tho they, above all things, drew us to
him and taught us to imitate him: "Take my
yoke upon you, and learn of me, for I am
meek and lowly in heart" (Matt. 11:29).

Humility makes our lives acceptable to God, meekness makes us acceptable to men. Balm, as I said before, sinking to the bottom of all liquids, is a figure of humility; and oil, floating as it does to the top, is a figure of gentleness and cheerfulness, rising above all things, and excelling all things, the very flower of love, which, so says St. Bernard, comes to perfection when it is not merely patient, but gentle and cheerful. Give heed, then, beloved, that you keep this mystic chrism of gentleness and humility in your heart, for it is a favorite device of the enemy to make people content with a fair outside semblance of these graces, not examining their inner hearts, and so fancying themselves to be gentle and humble while they are far otherwise. And this is easily perceived, because, in spite of their ostentatious gentleness and humility, they are stirred up with pride and anger by the smallest wrong or contradiction. There is a popular belief that those who take the antidote commonly called "St. Paul's gift," do not suffer from the viper's bite, provided, that is, that the remedy be pure; and even so true gentleness and humility will avert the burning and swelling which contradiction is apt to excite in our hearts. If, when stung by slander or ill-nature, we wax proud and swell with anger, it is a proof that our gentleness and humility are unreal, and mere artificial show. When the Patriarch Joseph sent his brethren back from Egypt to his father's house, he only gave them one counsel, "See that ye fall not out by the way" (Gen. 45:24). And so, my friends, say I to you. This miserable life is but the road to a blessed life; do not let us fall out by the way one with another; let us go on with the company of our brethren gently, peacefully, and kindly. Most emphatically I say it, if possible, fall out with no one, and on no pretext whatever suffer your heart to admit anger and passion. St. James says, plainly and unreservedly, that "the wrath of man worketh not the righteousness of God" (James 1:20). Of course it is a duty to resist evil and to repress the faults of those for whom we are responsible, steadily and firmly but gently and quietly. Nothing so stills the elephant when enraged as the sight of a lamb; nor does anything break the force of a cannon ball so well as wool. Correction given in anger, however tempered by reason, never has so much effect as that which is given altogether without anger; for the reasonable soul being naturally subject to reason, it is a mere tyranny which subjects it to passion, and whereinsoever reason is led by passion it becomes odious, and its just rule obnoxious. When a monarch

visits a country peaceably the people are gratified and flattered; but if the king has to take
his armies through the land, even on behalf of
the public welfare, his visit is sure to be un-
welcome and harmful, because, however
strictly military discipline may be enforced,
there will always be some mischief done to
the people. Just so when reason prevails,
and administers reproof, correction, and punishment in a calm spirit, altho it be strict,
every one approves and is content; but if reason be hindered by anger and vexation (which
St. Augustine calls her soldiers), there will be
more fear than love, and reason itself will be
despised and resisted. The same St Augustine, writing to Profuturus, says that it is
better to refuse entrance to any even the
least semblance of anger, however just; and
that because once entered in, it is hard to be
got rid of, and what was but a little mote soon
waxes into a great beam. For if anger tarries
till night, and the sun goes down upon our
wrath (a thing expressly forbidden by the
apostle, Eph. 4:26), there is no longer any
way of getting rid of it; it feeds upon endless
false fancies; for no angry man ever yet but
thought his anger just.

Depend upon it, it is better to learn how
to live without being angry than to imagine
one can moderate and control anger lawfully;

and if through weakness and frailty one is
overtaken by it, it is far better to put it away
forcibly than to parley with it; for give anger
ever so little way, and it will become your
master, like the serpent, who easily works in
its body wherever it can once introduce its
head. You will ask how to put away anger.
My child, when you feel its first movements,
collect yourself gently and seriously, not
hastily or with impetuosity. Sometimes in a
law court the officials who enforce quiet make
more noise than those they affect to hush;
and so, if you are impetuous in restraining
your temper, you will throw your heart into
worse confusion than before, and, amid the
excitement, it will lose all self-control.

Having thus gently exerted yourself, follow the advice which the aged St. Augustine
gave to a young bishop, Auxilius. "Do," said
he, "what a man should do." If you are like
the psalmist, ready to cry out, "Mine eye is
consumed for very anger," go on to say,
"Have mercy upon me, O Lord"; so that God
may stretch forth his right hand and control
your wrath. I mean, that when we feel stirred
with anger, we ought to call upon God for
help, like the apostles, when they were tossed
about with wind and storm, and he is sure
to say, "Peace, be still." But even here I
would again warn you that your very prayers

against the angry feelings which urge you
should be gentle, calm, and without vehe-
mence. Remember this rule in whatever reme-
dies against anger you may seek. Further,
directly you are conscious of an angry act,
atone for the fault by some speedy act of
meekness toward the person who excited your
anger. It is a sovereign cure for untruthful-
ness to unsay what you have falsely said at
once on detecting yourself in falsehood; and
so, too, it is a good remedy for anger to
make immediate amends by some opposite act
of meekness. There is an old saying, that
fresh wounds are soonest closed.

Moreover, when there is nothing to stir your
wrath, lay up a store of meekness and kindli-
ness, speaking and acting in things great and
small as gently as possible. Remember that
the Bride of the Canticles is described as
not merely dropping honey, and milk also,
from her lips, but as having it "under her
tongue" (Song of Solomon 4:11); that is to
say, in her heart. So we must not only speak
gently to our neighbor, but we must be filled,
heart and soul, with gentleness; and we must
not merely seek the sweetness of aromatic
honey in courtesy and suavity with strangers,
but also the sweetness of milk among those of
our own household and our neighbors; a sweetness terribly lacking to some who are as angels
abroad and devils at home!

SELECTIONS FROM

The Way to Christ, and the Supersensual Life; or, The Life Which Is Above Sense

BY

JAKOB BOEHME

JAKOB BOEHME

German mystic; born at Alt-Seidenberg, near
Görlitz, November, 1575; died at Görlitz, November 17, 1624. He learned the trade of shoemaker
in the little town of Seidenberg and at the same
time paid much attention to meditating on divine
things. He settled as master of his trade at
Görlitz in 1599. When he published his first book,
"Aurora," (a theosophic-philosophical account of
the universe), it was condemned by the authorities
at Görlitz. He was examined before a council and
dismissed on the promise that he would write no
more books, tho his friends urged him to continue
his productions, which circulated in manuscripts.
He wrote voluminously in German on such subjects as "The Three Principles of Divine Being";
"The Threefold Life of Man"; "Forty Questions
Concerning the Soul"; "True Penitence"; and "The
Way to Christ." A complete translation of his
works into English is in progress.

The Way From Darkness to True Illumination

There was a poor soul that had wandered out of paradise into that kingdom where the devil hath dominion; who drawing near, took it captive, and led it at his will. Placing joy and pleasure before it, he said, "Behold, now thou art great and powerful; endeavor to be greater and yet more powerful; display thy knowledge and wit, that thou mayest be admired, and get a great name in the world." The soul did as the devil counselled it, and yet knew not that he was its counsellor, but thought that it was guided by its own understanding, and that it did very well and right all the while. Going on in this course of life, it was met by our dear and loving Lord Jesus Christ, "who was manifested in our nature that he might destroy the works of the devil" (1 John 3:8). Speaking to it by a strong power, he discovered the way of salvation, and in his mercy called it to repentance; promising that he would then deliver it from that deformed image which it had gotten, and bring it into paradise again.

Now, when this spark of light divine was manifested in the soul, it saw itself, with its will and works, to be under the wrath of God and in his sight misshapen and deformed; and, in view of his just judgment, it fell into greatest anguish.

Upon this, the Lord Jesus spake unto it again with the voice of his grace; which induced it to seek to come before God, and entreat for mercy and the pardon of its sins; for it came to be strongly persuaded in itself that the satisfaction and atonement of Christ might avail for its deliverance. But the evil properties of the serpent, injected into the reason of the outward man, hindered the will of the soul, that it did not come before God; for, being of the world, it feared its reproach, in case it should disregard its honor and glory. Yet, this poor soul looked toward God, and desired grace from him, even that he would bestow his love upon it.

But when the devil saw that it thus prayed unto God and would enter into repentance, he again drew near; and thrusting carnal inclinations into its prayers, disturbed its good thoughts and desires, which prest toward God, drawing them back again to earthly things, that they might have no access to him.

Now altho the central will of the soul, indeed, sighed after God, yet the thoughts which had arisen in the mind were distracted, scattered, and destroyed. At this it was still more affrighted, and sought to pray more earnestly; but the devil, with his desire, awakened the evil properties slumbering within; so that sinful inclinations arose, and went into those things wherein before they had taken most pleasure and delight. The poor soul would fain go forward to God with its will, and therefore used all its endeavors; but its thoughts continually fled away from God into earthly things, and would not go to him.

Upon this, it bewailed itself before God; but was as if it were quite forsaken by him, and cast out from his presence. It could not get so much as one look of grace, but was in great anguish and fear; dreading every moment lest the wrath of God would be made manifest in giving it up to the devil. Thereupon, it fell into such great heaviness and sorrow that it became weary of all those temporal things which before had been its chief happiness and joy. It is true, the natural will still desired those things; but the soul would willingly leave them altogether, and desired to die to all temporal lust and joy whatsoever; longing only after its native country, from whence it originally came. But finding itself to be far from thence, in great distress and want, it knew not what to do; yet resolved to enter into itself and try to pray more earnestly.

But the devil opposing, withheld it, so that it could not bring itself into any greater fervency. He awakened the earthly lusts in the heart, that they might still keep their false right therein; setting them at variance with the new-born will and desire. For they would not die to their own will and light, but would still maintain their temporal pleasures; and so the poor soul was kept captive in its evil desires, that it could not stir, tho it still sighed and longed after the grace of God.

Thus did the devil "hinder its prayers" that it might not partake of divine strength; which caused it to think itself forsaken of God, not knowing that he was so near it with strong attraction. Also, gaining access to the soul, he mingled his desires with the earthly lusts of the flesh and tempted it; suggesting in its earthly thoughts, "Why dost thou pray; dost thou think that God regardeth thee? Do but consider what thoughts thou hast in his presence; are they not altogether evil? Thou hast no faith in God at all; how, then, should he hear thee? He heareth thee not." And, anon, he found suited to the case suggestions like these: "Why wilt thou needlessly vex thyself, since thou hast time enough to repent at leisure? Wilt thou be mad? I pray thee, do but look upon the world. Doth it not live in quiet and mirth? Yet it will be saved, notwithstanding all that; for hath not Christ paid the ransom, and satisfied for all men? Thou needest only persuade thyself that it is done for thee, and then thou shalt be saved. Thou canst not possibly in this world come to such enjoyment of God as thou seekest; therefore leave off this vain disquieting search, and take care for thy body, and look after temporal concerns, how thou mayest be advanced therein. What dost thou suppose will become of thee, if thou art so melancholy and grave? Thou wilt be the scorn of all, and they will laugh at thy folly; and so thou wilt spend thy days in mere sorrow and heaviness which is pleasing neither to God nor to nature. I pray thee, look upon the beauty of the world, which God hath created for thine enjoyment. Gather store of temporal goods beforehand, that thou mayest not be beholden to others or stand in need hereafter; and when old age cometh, or thou drawest near thine end, repent and prepare thyself for death, and God will receive thee then to heavenly mansions. Thus thou seest, there is no need of such ado, in vexing and stirring up thyself, as thou makest.''

In these and like thoughts the soul was ensnared, and brought into earthly desires, and so bound, as it were, with strong fetters and chains that it knew not what to do. For a moment it glanced at the world and the pleasures thereof, but still felt in itself a hunger after the grace of God. For he had touched and bruised it; and therefore it could not rest, but ever sighed to be rid of its sinful nature.

It yet did not attain unto true repentance, or even the knowledge or conviction of sin; tho it had a longing desire after such penitential sorrow. Being thus heavy and sad, it began to calculate as to what circumstances would most favor this work of true repentance, where it might be free from cares and the hindrances of the world, and also by what means it might win the favor of God.

At length, it purposed to betake itself to some solitary place and give over all worldly employments and temporal things; and hoped that by being bountiful to the poor, it should obtain God's mercy. Thus did it devise all ways for rest, and to gain the love and favor of God. But all would not avail; for the world still followed it in the lust of the flesh, and it was still ensnared in the devil's net. Tho for a little while it was somewhat cheered, yet presently it became as sorrowful as it was before. The truth was, it felt in itself the awakened wrath of God, yet knew not what it ailed.

Many times, great terror fell upon it, which

made it sick and faint with very fear; and
yet it knew not that Christ within was contending with Satan for its deliverance, nor
understood that its strong desire for penitence
came from Christ himself, by whom it was
thus drawn; neither did it know what hindered, that it could not yet attain to holiness
of feeling, nor see how fully it did bear the
image of the serpent, which gave the devil
all his power of access to it.

While in this state, by the providence of
God, this soul, afflicted and distrest, was
met by one regenerate and enlightened, who
asked: What aileth thee that thou art so rest-
less and troubled?

The distrest soul answered: The Creator
hath hid his countenance from me so that I can
not rest, nor do I know what I can do to gain
his loving-kindness. Mountains seem lying in
my way, which keep me from his grace; and
tho I ever sigh for him, yet I do not partake
of his virtue, power, and strength.

To this the enlightened soul replied: Thou
bearest Satan's image and art appareled like
himself: thus he hath entrance into thee, keeping thy will from sinking into God. For were
thy will thus lost in him, it would become
anointed with his power and strength in the
resurrection of our Lord Jesus Christ, which
unction would destroy thy monster form;

and thy first image, drawn in Paradise, would then revive within the center of thy soul, and, loosed from Satan's power, thou wouldst again be holy.

And because Satan envieth thee this happiness, which would then be thine, he fain would hold thee captive in fleshly lust; from which if thou art not delivered, thou must for ever be far from thy God.

Upon this, the poor afflicted soul stood terrified and silent; and would even have despaired of mercy, had not that gracious Being, who first awakened thoughts of himself, upheld it from despair. But still it wrestled in itself mid hope and doubt; for whatsoever hope built up, that doubt threw down again. Thus was it agitated with continual disquiet until the world and all its glory became loathsome, while worldly pleasures imparted no more joy, and yet it could not come to rest.

Again it met the soul enlightened, which finding it still in grief of mind inquired: Wilt thou destroy thyself in thy deep sorrow? Why dost thou torment thyself in thine own power and will? Since thou art but a worm, thy trouble doth thereby increase the more. Yea, with all thine utmost strivings thou wouldst not be released; for the more thou dost vex thyself with labor and sorrow,

the more painful thy nature will become, and
yet thou wilt not enter into rest. For thy
power is lost; and as a branch withered and
dead can not grow green and spring afresh
by its own power, so neither canst thou re-
gain thy place in God by thine own power
and strength; for thou art like the withered
plant which has become sapless and dead; and
in thy soul, if left unaided, will ever reign
continual strife.

Then the afflicted one inquired: What shall
I do that I may bud forth again, and recover
the image wherein man was first created?

The enlightened soul replied: Thou shalt
do nothing at all but forsake thine own will,
namely, that which thou callest I, or thyself.
By this means all thy evil properties will
grow weak, faint, and ready to die; and then
thou wilt be lost again in that one Being,
from whence thou didst originally spring.
Now, thou liest captive in the creatures: but
if thy will forsaketh them, these will die
in thee, with all their evil inclinations,
which at present do so hinder thy approach to God. If thou takest this course,
thy God will meet thee with his infinite love,
which he hath manifested in the incarnation
of our Lord Jesus Christ. Thus will sap, life,
and vigor be imparted to thee, whereby thou
mayest spring and flourish again, and as a

branch growing on the true vine, rejoice in the living God. So wilt thou recover the image of God, being delivered from that of the serpent; and thou shalt be "of the household of God," and have fellowship with angels.

But the poor soul said: How can I forsake my own will, so that I may die to the creature; seeing I must be in the world, and also have need of it as long as I live?

The enlightened soul answered: Since thou desirest me to tell thee, I must frankly declare that there is but one way to do it, which is "narrow and straight," and will be very hard and irksome to thee at the beginning; but afterward thou wilt walk in it cheerfully. Thou must seriously consider that in the course of this worldly life thou hast walked under the anger of God and upon the foundation of hell, and that this is not thy true native country, but that a Christian should and must live in Christ, and in his walking truly follow him; and that the kingdom of God can not come within him unless he be wholly subject to the spirit and power of Christ. Now, seeing "his kingdom is not of this world," thou must always be in a continual ascension toward heaven, if thou wilt follow Christ, tho thy body must dwell among the creatures and use them. Yet these only gain a form, and are kept alive, when thou re-

ceivest them into thy mind and desire. Then
they combine with the lusts that live in thy
natural life, and thereby thou art severed
from God; neither canst thou ever come to
live in him, unless thou so forsake these evils
of the creature, that they may indeed die in
thee. The narrow way, in which thou must
follow Christ in constant ascension, is in
despair of all thine own power and strength;
for in and by this thou canst make no ad-
vancement: and thou must firmly purpose
and resolve wholly to give thyself up to
the mercy of God, and to sink down with thy
whole mind and reason into the passion and
death of our Lord Jesus Christ; always desiring to persevere in the same, and to die
to all creatures therein. Thou must resolve
to put away from thee all unrighteousness and
whatsoever may hinder the freedom of thy
progress, keeping a watch over thy thoughts
and inclinations, that they admit no evil;
neither must thou suffer thyself to be ensnared by worldly esteem or profit. Thy
will must be wholly pure, and fixt in resolution never more to return to its idols, while
without delay thou must wholly separate from
them thy mind, and enter into the sincere way
of truth and righteousness, according to the
plain and full doctrine of Christ. And as
thou dost thus purpose to forsake the enemies

of thine own inward nature, so thou must
also forgive all thine outward enemies, re-
solving to meet them with love; that there
may be nothing left which shall be able to
separate thy soul from God; but that it may
be sincere and purged from all defilement.
Nay further, if God require it, thou must be
willing and ready to forsake all thy temporal
honor and profit, that thou mayest have
sympathy with Christ in his humiliation,
while thou regardest nothing that is earthly so
as to set upon it thy heart and affections.

In whatsoever condition thou art, as to
the world's regard, thou must esteem thyself
to be but a servant of God, or as a steward
in the office wherein thy Lord hath placed
thee. All self-exaltation must be brought
low; and so annihilated that nothing of
thine own or any other creature may stay in
thy will, to bring thy thoughts or desire to be
set upon it.

Thou must also, firmly impress on thy mind
that if, feeling thine own utter weakness, thou
comest to God with the desire and purpose
to repent which he himself hath given thee,
thou shalt certainly partake of the promised
grace through the merits of Jesus Christ,
namely—of his outflowing love; which indeed, if Christ is thine, is already in thee,
but will flow forth in exact proportion

to the power of faith with which thou
drawest thy supplies. This love possest will gain for thee deliverance from
all the creatures; while with will subdued thou shalt have victory over thy grand
adversary. But thou must ever bear in mind,
that thou canst neither will nor do anything
in thine own strength, but only enter into the
suffering and resurrection of Jesus Christ;
and taking them to thyself, thus to assault
and break in pieces, the kingdom of the devil
in thee and mortify the creatures.

Now when thou art thus returning, thy
heavenly Father will haste to meet thee at
thy coming; and with inward voice of sweet
assurance, proclaim that he hath ordered to
be put on thee, the best robe, spotless and
white; and for a seal of love, a ring upon thy
hand. Thus, for the sake of Jesus, he will
embrace thee with his Spirit; and thou shalt
have grace to pour before him thy confession,
and powerfully to pray. This thou wilt find
to be indeed the place of wrestling; and if
thou standest resolutely here, nor shrinkest
back, thou shalt see great wonders. For thou
shalt find Christ in thee assaulting hell and
crushing thy spiritual foes, which will cause
a great tumult within; also, undiscovered sins
will then awake, threatening to separate thee
for ever from thy God. Thus shalt thou truly

learn how death and life contend against each other; thou shalt understand by what passeth within thyself what heaven and hell are.

At all which, be not moved; for at length all the creatures in thee will grow faint and ready to die, and then thy will shall wax stronger and be able to subdue all evil inclinations. So shall thy soul daily ascend toward heaven, while by degrees thy earthly nature fadeth away, until finally thou shalt obtain a mind wholly renewed. Thus shalt thou be delivered from thy present anguish, and "return unto thy rest," according as God first designed for man—of which we read Ps. 116:7.

With such advice this soul, long desolate and tried, began to practise with such earnestness this course that it supposed it soon should gain the victory; but it had not learned as yet to lay aside all of its own working; so it continued to feel as if it were rejected and forsaken of God, and received from him not so much as one look or glimpse of his grace. And herein was fulfilled, that which was written (Rom. 9:31, 32), "Israel, which followed after the law of righteousness hath not attained to the law of righteousness. Wherefore? Because they sought it not by faith, but as it were, by the works of the law."

This led the soul to say to itself: Surely, thou hast not sincerely submitted to God. Desire nothing at all of him, but only submit thyself to his judgment, that he may destroy thy evil inclinations. Sink down into him beyond the limits of nature and the creature, that he may do with thee what he will; for thou art not worthy to speak to him. Accordingly it resolved to sink down, forsaking its own will; which having done, there fell upon it presently the deepest repentance for the sins it had committed, while it bitterly bewailed the estrangement of its heart from God, which should have borne his image. And because of its sorrow, it could no longer give utterance to words when it came before God; but lying in the dust, it dwelt upon the bitter passion and death of Christ; what great anguish he had suffered for its sake, that it might be delivered out of its anguish and changed into the image of God.

In this consideration, it wholly sunk down, and did nothing but confess its own past blindness and neglect, and its ingratitude to God, in slighting the great love which he had shown it while it had been so much affected with earthly things. It lamented that by reason of its carnal inclinations it must now, overwhelmed with shame, lie captive in its sin and misery until the Lord should come in mercy for its deliverance. As it was thus sighing and bowed down, it was drawn into an abyss of horror, was laid, as it were, at the gates of hell, and left as if to perish. Upon which this poor, troubled soul, seeming now wholly forsaken, was almost bereft of sense, and, in despair of itself, ceased from its own workings and would willingly have become annihilated. Accordingly, it did yield itself entirely, and desired nothing else but to die into the death of its Redeemer, who had passed through this for it. In this dying state, it began to sigh and pray in itself very inwardly, and to sink down into God's mere mercy. And now suddenly was lifted on it the loving countenance of God; which, penetrating through it as a great light, made it exceedingly joyful. It then began to pray aright, thanking the Most High for such grace; and to rejoice abundantly, that it was delivered from the anguish of hell. Now, it tasted of the sweetness to be found in "the way of holiness" and in God's word of promise; and all the evil spirits which before harassed it, keeping it back from this grace, love, and inward presence of God, were forced to depart. "The marriage of the Lamb," spoken of in Rev. 19:7, was now solemnized with this soul which he had betrothed to himself; and the seal ring of Christ's victory was

placed upon it, now that it was received to be
the child and heir of God again.

When this was done, the soul became most
joyful; and began to work in this new power,
and with praise to celebrate God's wonders;
and it thought to walk, henceforth, in the
same light, joy and strength.

But it was soon assaulted, from without
by the world's reproach, and from within by
great temptation; so that it was led to ques-
tion whether its foundation had been laid in
God, and if it had really partaken of such
grace. For the "accuser of the brethren"
came to it, who would fain lead it from this
course, and make it doubtful whether, indeed,
it were in such close union with its God;
whispering thus to it inwardly: "This
happy change of feeling is not from the Lord,
but only of thine own imagining:"

Also, the divine light retired within the
soul, shining but in the inward ground—
as fire raked up in embers; so that reason was
perplexed, while the soul knew not what had
wrought this change, and almost feared that it
was now forsaken, not having truly "tasted
of the heavenly gift," respecting which we
read, Heb. 6:4. Yet, it could not leave off
struggling; for the burning fire of love divine
was kindled in it, which produced within a
strong, enduring thirst after its God. So it

humbled itself in his presence, who enabled it to pray aright, and by heart searchings to put away all evil inclinations.

This process was severe and painful; making the body faint and weak, as if it had been sick.

Now, when the poor soul saw that it was derided by the world because it walked no longer in the way of wickedness and vanity; and also, that it was inwardly assaulted by the accuser, Satan, who continually placed before it earthly considerations, that he might ensnare it, from its inmost soul it cried: Oh, God! what shall I now do, to come to rest?

While it was thus perplexed, the enlightened soul met it again, and said: What aileth thee, my brother, that thou art so sad?

The distrest one replied: I have followed thy counsel, and thereby attained a ray of divine light; but it is gone from me again, and I am now deserted. Moreover, I have, outwardly, very great trials, being forsaken of former friends, while within I am assaulted with doubt and anguish, and know not what to do.

Then the enlightened soul exclaimed: I now rejoice for thee; for plainly I perceive that our beloved Lord is leading thee, in richest grace, through that pilgrimage and process which correspondeth to his own while in this world. He was continually depised and slandered and had no treasure here; and now his badge thou wearest. Nor think it strange; for thou must be tried, that thou mayest be refined and purified. In this distress thou wilt be constrained to hunger and to cry after deliverance, and by such prayer thou wilt attract from heaven rich supplies. And if amid the trees of God's own planting thou wouldst grow and flourish, thy growth must be promoted, both from above and from beneath; just as a young tree endureth in its season both heat and cold, while it deriveth strength even from the wind which sweepeth over it with its rough blast. Yet, this is an hour wherein, as Christ's valiant soldier, thou must stand unflinching. For now, the eternal Father would bring forth in thee, in full proportions, the image of his Son, for which thy soul must travail; but soon thou shalt bud forth, from the Vine, Christ, and in his vineyard bear abundant fruit. Thus thou shalt become indeed the Holy Spirit's temple; to which inquiring souls shall gather to learn from thy experience eternal truth.

Since then 'tis only thus that paradise can spring again in thee, be not dismayed amid temptations; for Satan fiercely striveth to retain the kingdom which he once possest in thee. Yet he must now depart confounded;

for it hath been taken by One who is "stronger than the strong man armed"; of which we read, Luke 11: 21, 22. But thou wilt find that "thy life, now hid with Christ in God," spoken of in Col. 3: 3, will not be judged aright by those who are of earth; while yet, with thy new birth, thy spirit is in unison with those in heaven. Therefore be patient and "wait upon the Lord, that hideth his face"; as in Isa. 8: 17, and whatsoever shall befall thee, take it from his hands, as all designed and working for thy highest good.

After this counsel, the enlightened soul departed; and the inquiring one pursued its course under the patient suffering of Christ; and, depending solely upon the imparted strength and power of God, entered into hope. Thenceforth it daily gained in strength; while from within, its evil inclinations fading away, it attained to a high state of grace, realizing already in itself the coming of God's kingdom; and lying low before its God, were opened to it by the Spirit the gates of revelation. Concerning this, we read, 1 Cor. 2.

Thus did this soul, long tempest-tossed, arrive at length through faith and prayer to its true rest in God; to which may he, in mercy infinite, bring all who fain would know him.

Jakob Boehme

A Discourse Between the Scholar and His Master Upon Heaven and Hell

The scholar asked his master, Whither goeth the soul, when the body dieth? His master answered, There is no necessity for it to go anywhere.

What, nowhere! said the scholar, in amazement; must not the soul leave the body at death, and go either to heaven or hell?

The master replied: The outward, mortal life, with the body, shall separate themselves from the soul; but it hath heaven and hell within itself before; according as it is written (Luke 17: 20, 21): "The kingdom of God cometh not with observation; neither shall they say, lo here! or lo there! for behold, the kingdom of God is within you." Therefore, whichever is manifested in it, during this earthly life, in that it remaineth fixt after its release from the body; according as we read (Rev. 22: 11), "He that is unjust, let him be unjust still; and he that is filthy, let him be filthy still; and he that is righteous, let him be righteous still; and he that is holy, let him be holy still."

This is hard to understand, said the scholar, for I had supposed it must go to some unknown place.

173

But the master said: No verily, there is
no such kind of entering in, either to heaven
or hell; for God is in heaven, and yet is everywhere. And the devil is in hell; and "the
whole world," as the apostle hath taught us,
"lieth in wickedness" (1 John 5 : 19), or "in
the wicked one" (according to verse 18).
Thus, in a sense, hell is everywhere, as well
as heaven.

The scholar, startled hereat, said, Pray
make me to understand this.

Then thou must understand, replied the
master, what heaven is. It is the turning of
the will into the love of God. Wheresoever
thou findest God manifesting himself in love,
there thou findest heaven, without traveling
for it, so much as one foot. Also by this thou
mayest understand what and where hell is.
I say unto thee, it is the turning of the will
into the wrath of God. Wheresoever the anger
of God doth more or less manifest itself—
there certainly, is more or less of hell, in
whatsoever place it be—mark it well. And
this cometh to pass first in the present life,
whereof St. Paul, speaking of his fellow
Christians, saith, "Our conversation is in
heaven" (Phil. 3 : 20). All, therefore, doth
consist in the entering of the will into heaven
—by hearing the voice of Christ, and thus
knowing and following him. And so also it is,

on the other hand. Understandest thou this?

The scholar replied, I think I do in part. But how cometh the will thus to enter into heaven?

On this point, I will endeavor to satisfy thee, said his master; but thou must be very attentive to what I shall say. Know then, my son, that when the ground of the will yieldeth itself unto God, then it sinketh out of its own self, into a certain unseen deep, where God only is manifest and where he alone worketh and willeth. Thus it becometh nothing to itself, as to its own working and willing; "For it is God which worketh in it, both to will and to do, of his good pleasure" (Phil. 2:13). God dwells in this resigned will, by which the soul is sanctified and so enabled to come into divine rest.

Now in this case, when the body dieth, the soul is so thoroughly penetrated with the divine love and so illuminated with divine light, even as a glowing hot iron is by the fire, that it loseth its darkness and becometh bright and shining. God's love alone inhabiteth that soul, being in it a shining light and a new, glorious life. This is the entering of the will into heaven.

Be pleased sir, to proceed, said the scholar, and let me know how it fareth on the other side.

The ungodly soul, said the master, is not willing in this life-time to enter into the will of God, but goeth on still in its own lust and desire, in vanity and falsehood, and so entereth into the will of the devil. It receiveth thereupon into itself nothing but wickedness, nothing but deceit, pride, covetousness, envy and wrath, and thereinto it giveth up its will and whole desire. Having thus "yielded itself, to be the servant of sin," this worketh therein; even as the love of God doth in the regenerate will, and penetrateth it throughout, as fire doth iron; and it is not possible for this soul to come into the rest of God, because God's anger is manifested in it. And when the body is parted from it, then beginneth the eternal melancholy and despair; because it now findeth that it is become altogether vanity, even a vanity most vexatious to itself, and a distracting fury, a self-tormenting abomination. Now it perceiveth itself disappointed of every thing which it had before fancied; and blind, naked and wounded, hungry and thirsty, without the least prospect of being ever relieved or obtaining so much as one drop of the water of eternal life. Also, it feeleth itself to be a mere devil and its own executioner and tormentor, and, affrighted at its own dark image, it would fain flee from itself, yet can not, being fast bound with the chains of that dark nature whereinto it had sunk itself when in the flesh. And, being confounded at its own nakedness and vileness, it would, were it possible, hide itself from the majesty of God and cover its abominable form from his most holy eye, even tho it were by casting itself still deeper into darkness. Such a soul is itself but mere wrath, having by its false desire, which it had awakened in itself, comprehended and shut up itself therewith, and so transformed itself into the nature and property thereof. And since also the light of God does not shine within nor his love incline it, there is experienced that which is predicted in Jude 13, even "the blackness of darkness for ever." Also it carrieth about within itself an anxious fire-source, which is its hell; nor is it able to discern the least glimpse of the light of God or to feel the least spark of his love. Thus it needeth no entering into hell or being carried thither; for in whatsoever place it be, so long as it is in itself, it is in hell. And tho it should travel far from its present place, yet still would it remain in the hellish source and darkness.

If this be so, said the scholar, how then cometh it that a holy soul doth not in this life perfectly perceive the heavenly light and joy; and that he who is "without God in the world" doth not also here feel hell, as well as hereafter? Why should they not both be perceived and felt, as well in this life as in the next seeing that both of them are in man, while one or the other worketh in every one?

To this the master answered: The kingdom of heaven in the saints is built up and manifested through faith. They who have God within them and live by his Spirit find the kingdom of God in their faith, and thereby feel his love; by which faith also the will hath given up itself into God, and is made one with his. In a word, all is transacted within them by faith, which is to them "the evidence of things not seen" (Heb. 11:1). But their natural life is nevertheless encompassed with flesh and blood; and this standing in a contrariety thereto—being placed through man's fall under God's anger and environed about with the world, which by no means can be reconciled to faith—these faithful souls can not but be very much exposed to attacks from this world, wherein they are sojourners; neither can they be insensible to being thus compassed about with this world's vain lust, which ceaseth not continually to beset this outward, mortal life, and to tempt them in manifold ways, even as it did Christ. Whence the world on one side and the devil on the other, together with indwelling sin, do thoroughly penetrate and sift it; whereby it cometh to pass that the soul is often in anxiety when these three are all set upon her together, assaulting her life. But hereupon she sinketh down into the hope of God's grace, and standeth like a beautiful rose in the midst of thorns, until released therefrom by the death of the body; when she will have henceforth nothing to hinder her growth in holiness. And even during this life she may "walk with God": as it is recorded of Enoch (Gen. 5:22); while the Spirit penetrating her throughout with divine love delivereth her out of her own hell, changing it into heaven.

But thou also askest, Why do not those who are without God, feel hell in this world? I answer: They bear it about with them in their wicked consciences, yet know it not, because the world hath blinded their eyes, and its deadly intoxicating cup hath cast them into a most fatal sleep. Notwithstanding this, it must be owned that the wicked do frequently feel hell within them during the time of this mortal life, tho they may not apprehend what it is because of the earthly vanity which cleaveth unto them, and the pleasures and amusements of sense wherewith they are intoxicated. Moreover, it is to be noted that the outward life in every such one, hath yet the light of the outward nature wherewith it is

ruled; and so long as it is thus, the pain of
hell can not be revealed. But when the body
dieth, and the soul can no longer enjoy such
temporal pleasure and delight nor the light of
this outward world—which, as to itself, is
wholly thereupon extinguished—then it
stands in an eternal hunger and thirst after
such vanities with which it was here in love;
while yet it can reach nothing but that false
will which it had imprest in itself while in
the body, and wherein it had been gratified
to its great loss. And now, whereas it had
too much of its will in this life and yet was
not contented therewith, it hath, after this
separation by death, comparatively so little of
it, which createth within it this everlasting
thirst after that which it can never more obtain.

Thus is it in a perpetual anxious lust after
vanity, according to its former life; and in
a constant rage of hunger, after those ways of
wickedness wherein it was immersed while in
the flesh. Fain would it do more evil still
but that it hath no longer either wherein or
wherewith to effect the same, and therefore
it doth perform this only in itself. All is
now internally transacted as if it were outward, and so the ungodly soul is tormented by
those furies which are in his own mind. He
is verily become his own tormentor. This

hellish hunger and thirst could not be fully manifested within till the body, which ministered to the soul in all its cravings that for which it lusted, be stript off.

I perceive then, said the scholar, that the soul having, while in the body, lived according to the lusts thereof, still retaineth the very same inclinations and affections which it had before, altho it no longer hath opportunity or capacity to satisfy them; and that as this can not be, there is then hell manifested in that soul, which had been shut up in it before, by means of the outward life in the flesh and of the light of this world. On the other hand, I clearly perceive, by what I have heard, that heaven can not but be in a loving soul which is possest of God and hath subdued thereby the body to the obedience of the Spirit in all things, having perfectly immersed itself into the will and love of God. And when the body dieth, and this soul is hence redeemed from earth (it is now evident to me), the life of God, which was in a measure hidden in it, will display itself gloriously, and heaven consequently be then manifested. Do I rightly understand?

The master answered, It is very rightly understood by you. Every created, intellectual being remaineth in its own principle, whether it be of light or of darkness; and therein it is conscious of the presence of God, who is everywhere, whether in love or in wrath. Accordant with this is the sentiment in Ps. 139:8-12: "If I ascend up into heaven, thou art there; if I make my bed in hell, behold, thou art there. If I take the wings of the morning, and dwell in the uttermost parts of the sea, even there shall thy hand lead me, and thy right hand shall hold me. If I say, surely, the darkness shall cover me, even the night shall be light about me. Yea, the darkness hideth not from thee, but the night shineth as the day: the darkness and the light are both alike to thee."

If the soul be in the love of God, then it beholdeth him accordingly, and feeleth that he "is love." But if it hath captivated itself in his wrath, then it can not behold him otherwise than as a "God of vengeance." To it, all places are alike, if in God's love; and if it be not there, every place is a hell unto it; for what can bound a thought? Thus, with every intellectual being, whether of the order of angels or of human souls, the state of each is fixt by its own character; in which condition he may consequently very well be said to be in "his own place"; as in Acts 1:25.

I remember, replied the scholar, that it is written concerning the great traitor that he went after death to his own place.

The same is true, said the master, of every soul when it departeth this mortal life; each abideth in its own principle and in its own property, or, as in the words of Scripture, in "its own place."

The divine nature, of which the angels are partakers, is communicated to the spirits redeemed from earth: but the appropriation or participation thereof is different to every one, according as each hath attracted the same by his desire. And what I have here said of the divine is no less to be considered in the participation of the diabolical nature, or the "power of darkness," as to the manifold modes, degrees, and appropriations thereof. Moreover, remember well that heaven and hell are in us at strife, in the time of this life: where thou dost not dwell, as to thy selfhood and to thine own will, there the holy angels dwell with thee, and every where about thee. On the contrary, where thou dwellest as to thyself, in self-seeking and self-will, there be sure Satan will be round about thee, and take up his abode within. Which may God in his mercy prevent.

I understand not this, said the scholar, so perfectly as I could wish. Be pleased therefore, to make it a little more clear to my mind.

So the master proceeded: Mark well what

I say. Where God willeth in any creature,
there is he manifested; and in consequence of
this very manifestation of himself, the angels
delight to dwell about' that soul. But where
the will of the creature is not actuated by the
will of God, he is not manifested to it, nor
can he be. Neither do the angels "encamp
round about" such an one; for they dwell
only where is seen the glory of God, and serve
to increase the manifestation of this glory.
What then doth dwell in such an one, since he
is forsaken both of God and angels? The
case is evidently this: in that soul, where the
will acteth contrary to the will of God, Satan
dwelleth, and with him all of evil. Would that
this truth were laid to heart.

It is possible, said the scholar, I may seem
to ask needless and, it may be, improper questions: but I beseech you, good sir, to have
patience with me in my ignorance; for I have
several questions still to propose, while I am
almost ashamed to name them.

Be plain with me, replied his master, and
suggest whatever is upon your mind; yea, be
not ashamed, even to appear ridiculous, so
that by querying you may but become wiser.

The scholar, grateful for this liberty, inquired, How far then, are heaven and hell
asunder?

As far as day and night, answered the

master. Heaven appeareth only through the manifestation of God, who is thus gloriously manifested in the souls of the sanctified. Heaven is nothing else but a revelation of the eternal one, wherein all the working and willing is in a quiet love. So in like manner it is with the world of despair, which appeareth in that wherein the foundation of hell is manifested, namely, in self and in the perverted and unsanctified will. The visible world hath both in it; but man, during the time of this life, seeth not the spiritual world. For the outward world, with its substance, is a cover to the spiritual, even as is the body to the soul. But when the outward man dieth, then the spiritual world is manifested; and this, either in the eternal light with holy angels, or with evil spirits in eternal darkness.

Both angels and human souls spring from the same origin, even from the divine will and wisdom; yet some remain in light, while others have entered into darkness. This darkness cometh from the receiving of self-desire and light, from union of the human will with God's. And wheresoever there is this willing with God, the love of God is undoubtedly in the working, and his light will not fail to manifest itself—constituting heaven; for heaven and hell are but a manifestation of the divine will, either in light or darkness, in love or in wrath.

A Prayer of Henry W. Foote

Infinite and holy one, whom we know as our Father and the Father of our Lord Jesus Christ, we devoutly thank thee for the mercy that created us from the dust, and for the greater mercy that has created us anew by a heavenly adoption as thy children. For the undying yearnings, which thou hast implanted in us, after things unseen, for their satisfaction in thyself, we thank thee; and we rejoice that thou hast been willing to encourage our frail and mortal spirits, by revealing to us something of the perfection of thy nature and calling us to follow after thee. Grant, we pray, that thy loving-kindness may be followed by our obedience. And do thou so confirm our best purposes by renewing our sense of thy presence, that we may both imitate thy nature and accept thy dealings with us in the spirit of childlike trust, by the help of thy dear Son, Jesus Christ our Lord. AMEN.

The Excellence of a Meek and Quiet Spirit

AND

A Prayer

BY

BENJAMIN WHICHCOTE, D.D.

BENJAMIN WHICHCOTE (WHITCHCOTE)

One of the principal founders of the Latitudinarian school of divines in England, was born at Stoke, Shropshire, May 4, 1609; died at Cambridge, May, 1683. He was admitted a pensioner of Emmanuel College, Cambridge, in 1626 (B.A., 1629; M.A. and fellow, 1633), and was ordained in 1636. He was appointed Sunday afternoon lecturer at Trinity College, a post which he held for twenty years, and through the work done there was best known to his contemporaries. In 1643 he was preferred to the college living of North Cadbury in Somersetshire, but in the following year was recalled to Cambridge as provost of King's. In 1649 he resigned the living of North Cadbury, and was presented to that of Milton in Cambridgeshire, which he retained till his death. At the Restoration he was ejected from his headship, but adhered to the church when the Act of Uniformity was passed, held the cure of St. Anne's, Blackfriars, from 1662 until the church was burned in the great fire of 1666, and that of St. Lawrence, Jewry, from 1668. His principal works (all posthumous) are: "Some Select Notions of that Learned and Reverend Divine of the Church of England, Benj. Whichcote, D.D.," (1685); "A Treatise of Devotion, with Morning and Evening Prayer for all the Days of the Week" (1697); "Select Sermons" (1698), "Several Discourses" (1701); "The True Notion of Place in the Kingdom or Church of Christ" (1717); "The Works of the Learned Benjamin Whichcote" (1751); "Moral and Religious Aphorisms" (1753).

The Excellence of a Meek and Quiet Spirit

[The ornament of a meek and quiet spirit, which is in the sight of God of great price.—1 Pet. 3:4.]

We find it is in vain for any one to attempt to purge the stream, unless he first cleanse the fountain. You must begin at the spring-head. The heart is the principle of action. Life begins there; and motion is from thence. It is that which first lives, and last dies. Our Savior tells us that what proceeds out of the mouth comes from the heart, and so defiles a man. For, from thence come evil thoughts, murders, blasphemies, etc. (Matt. 15:18), and (Matt. 5:28) our Savior tells us of the adultery of the heart. And (Matt. 12:34) "Out of the abundance of the heart," etc., and verse 35: "A good man, out of the good treasury of his heart, bringeth forth good things," etc. Men show their spirits by their words and actions: and these are as they are meant, and intended. The greatest performance in the life of man, is the government of his spirit. So (Prov. 25:28; comp. 16:32), "He that is slow to anger, is better than the mighty: and he that ruleth his own spirit, than he that taketh a city."

189

He that doth subdue the motion of irregular passion, doth a greater matter than he who conquers nations, or beats down walls and bulwarks. Therefore give me the man, of whom I may say: this is the person, who in "the true use of reason (the perfection of human nature), who in the practise and exercise of virtue (its accomplishment), hath brought himself into such a temper as is co-natural to those principles, and warranted thereby." Of all other men I may say that they have neglected their chief business, and have forgot the great work that was in their hand, and what ought chiefly to be done in the world. For, the greatest thing that lies upon every one to do, is the regulating of his own mind and spirit. And he that hath not done this hath been in the world to little purpose. For, this is the business of life; to inform our understandings, to refine our spirits; and, then, to regulate the actions of our lives: to settle, I say, such a temper of mind as is agreeable to the dictates of sober reason and constituted by the graces of the divine Spirit.

Now that I may give you an account of this in the text, this meek and quiet spirit, I must do it by looking into the state and operation of it. Through meekness, a man hath always fair weather within. Through meekness, he gives no manner of offense or disturbance any where abroad. And, in particular, I may say these (following) several things of the meek and quiet spirit.

First: There is no ungrounded passion; no boisterous motion; no exorbitancy, nothing of fury. No perplexity of mind, nor over-thoughtfulness. Men that are thus disquieted know not what to do, can give no answer, nor can resolve on anything. No confusion of thought; for that is darkness within, and brings men into such disorder that they know not what is before them. No eagerness of desire; no impetuosity. They do not say with her in the Scripture, ''Give me children, or else I die'' (Gen. 30:1). No respect to God or man will quiet or moderate such spirits, if they have not what they are bent upon. No inordinancy of appetite; but so as always to be governed according to the measures and rules of reason and virtue. No partiality or self-flattery. One of a meek spirit does not over-value himself. Those of the contrary temper are always putting themselves into a fool's paradise, conceiting above what there is sense or reason for. No impotent self-will. He that gives way to self-will is an enemy to his own peace, and is the great disturber of the world; he is an anti-God, imposeth upon God himself, and is within no law. And (in the last place) no fond self-love. All these are verities of this meek and quiet spirit. And these are great things and tend to happiness, are suitable to our state, becoming the relation we stand in to God and to one another. The meek in temper are freed from all those internal dispositions that cause a great deal of unquietness in the world. For, as mischievous as the world either is, or is thought to be, our sufferings from abroad, all the injuries that we meet with from without are neither so great nor so frequent as the annoyances that arise from discomposure of our own minds and from inward malignity. I say, that they who complain so much of the times and of the world may learn this; that the sufferings from injurious dealings from any without us are nothing in comparison to those we find from within. For this inward malady doth altogether disable the senses and succors of reason. This is a constant malady; and by this self-enjoyment is made very uncertain. This is the first thing, that through meekness of spirit we are always in a calm, have fair weather within our own breasts, and do arrive to a good state of health and settlement.

Secondly: Through this meekness of spirit, there is good carriage and behavior toward others. The meek are never injurious or cen-

sorious, but are ready to take in good part,
and make the best construction that the case
will bear. They will account other men's
faults rather their infirmity than their crime;
and they look upon the harm done them by
others to be rather inadvertency than design
—rather contingent ill accidents than bad
meaning. The meek man is a good neighbor,
a good friend; a credit to religion, one that
governs himself according to reason, makes
no injury by any misconstruction, and, in
case of any wrong done, sits down with easy
satisfaction. How much do men differ upon
account of moderation, meekness, and fair-
ness? We find, upon our ordinary application to some persons, that they will admit any
reasonable and fair proposal; be ready to
hear and take in good part; are of easy
access, fair conditioned, easy to be entreated:
but others there are of so bad a condition that
you may come twenty times to them, before
you find them in a good mood, or fit to be
dealt withal. They are seldom in so good a
disposition that an indifferent proposal may be
made to them. But for those that are of
meek and quiet spirits, I may say of such
persons either that they are very ready to
grant what is desired, or else, if they do deny,
it shall be upon such grounds of reason as
will satisfy.

But because things are best known by their
contraries, I will show you who those persons are of whom it can not be said, that they
are of meek and quiet spirits; to wit, the
proud, the arrogant, insolent, haughty, presumptuous, self-confident, and assuming. For
these are boisterous, stormy, tempestuous,
clamorous. These persons will put themselves
and others, as much as they can, into a flame.
These are the disturbers of mankind; and
their neighbors are rid of a burden, when
they are removed. What storms and tempests
are in the world natural, these are in the world
moral. Earthquakes, storms, and tempests,
do not lay more heavy upon the world natural
than these men do upon the world of mankind. But meekness doth so qualify the soil
where it is, that all the moral virtues will
there thrive and prosper; such as humility,
modesty, patience, ingenuity, candor. But
malice and envy are the worst of vices, being
the greatest degeneracy and participation of
the devilish nature. These have no place in
this meek and quiet spirit.

Lastly, I add that an ill-natured person
is altogether uncapable of happiness. If,
therefore, it hath been any one's lot either to
have been born or bred to an ill-nature, I say
in this case, he is more concerned to apply a
remedy than he that hath received a deadly

wound, or is bodily sick, hath to apply himself to the chirurgeon, or to the physician, lest his wound or disease should prove mortal. For these inward maladies will otherwise prove fatal to his soul; and the only remedy to be applied is self-reflection, due consideration, self-examination, and the exercise and practise of virtue.

Observe, now, the incompetency of the world's judgment. How fond and partial is the world, who do applaud the great disturbers of mankind, such as make havoc and desolation in the family of God, bring in confusion, and turn all into hurly-burly giving to such as these titles of honor; naming them conquerors and victorious persons! How fond (I say) and partial is the world; who do so magnify the fame of high-spirited, turbulent, self-willed persons! thinking them men of courage and resolution: and, on the other hand, accounting the innocent and harmless to be persons of no spirit or activity. Where as the greatest sign of power and bravest performance in the life of man is to govern his own spirit, and to subdue his passions. And, this, if the Scripture may give judgment, is the greatest ornament belonging to a man, and that which is the most valued by God, from whose judgment there is no appeal. "The ornament of a meek and quiet spirit, which is in the sight of God of great price." And, good old Jacob, when leaving the world, when about to bless his posterity, he came to Simeon and Levi; remembering their horrid cruelty, it puts him to a loss; "O my soul, come not thou into their secret, for instruments of cruelty are in their habitation," etc. (Gen. 49:5, 6). Things are very differently accounted above and below. And by this it appears that the guise of the world and the fancy of men are the most impotent and fond things imaginable.

And further yet, as to the judgment of Scripture in this case: This is the true temper of religion, and prophesied of the gospel-state (Isa. 11:6 and 65:25). Our Savior, in his beatitudes (Matt. 5), begins with this spirit. And, that this is the temper that shall rule and prevail in the gospel-state, consult these Scriptures (Eph. 4:2; 1 Tim. 6:11). A man can not speak a good thing, without meekness. If he speaks of God, of matters of reason and religion, he spoils that which he meddles with, if he be not meek. For we must in meekness instruct those that oppose themselves (2 Tim. 2:25). No good notion will take place, no good seed can be sown, no plant will thrive; every thing that is divine and heavenly will vanish, if it be not settled by this temper. "Who is a wise man, and endued with knowledge among you; let him show, out of a good conversation, his works, with meekness of wisdom" (James 1:21; 3:13). Wisdom is not, but in conjunction with meekness (1 Pet. 3:15). There is no religious disposition, or good conversation, where it is not. Meekness must accompany all motions in religion, or else 'tis passion, or a man's own interest. Without this, we are out of God's way, and have not his blessing (Ps. 25:9). And this is that qualification that makes us capable of the promises of the gospel. Tho this temper be accounted by the incompetent world a kind of sheepishness, and such as these are thought to be persons of no mettle nor spirit; yet the Holy Spirit reckons otherwise. See how the Scripture reckons of Moses; of whom it is said, he was the meekest man upon earth (Num. 12:3), and yet a person of great courage and resolution. How doth he appear to Pharaoh, to his face, tho threatened by Pharaoh, who was a man of the greatest power? How did he act in the greatest dangers? Yet, of this Moses, of whom the greatest performances are recorded, it is said that he was the meekest man upon earth. We read of the Messias, that the Spirit of the Lord shall rest upon him; the spirit of counsel and might.

With righteousness he shall judge the poor; and reprove with equity, for the meek of the earth (Isa. 11 : 2; 61 : 1). These are acts of authority and power; and thus is the Messiah declared. Consider also that St. Paul useth the meekness of our Savior for an argument to persuade others to that temper. I beseech you by the meekness and gentleness of Christ (2 Cor. 10 : 1). And (Matt. 11 : 29) our Savior saith, "Learn of me; for I am meek and lowly in heart." From all that I have said, it doth appear very reasonable that we should appeal from the judgment and sentence of worldly spirited men, who applaud persons that are of venturous undertakings, of fierce resolutions, of impotent passions, and unreasonable affections.

Wherefore let every man, in the first place, look after his home work—what he hath to do at home—to establish in himself a due frame and temper of mind; for, till this be done, he is not fit to walk abroad, or to have to do with others. When this is done, then there will be patient forbearance and making allowance. This is that which the apostle adviseth (Gal. 6 : 1): "Brethren, if any man be overtaken in a fault; ye which are spiritual, restore such an one, in the spirit of meekness, considering thyself, lest thou also be tempted." If any one do us an injury,

and transgress, let us make him that allowance that God makes us; let us make him an
abatement for the weakness of his nature,
and for the multiplicity of his principles; for
that government that he is charged withal. It
may be, he may be at odds with himself, and
his inferior appetites in rebellion and confusion: and it must be some time before he
can recover himself, and bring things into
order again in his family. God allows for
this; and we should allow for it, in one
another.

'Tis necessary, when ever we have to do
with one another, that there should be given
fair allowance and consideration of men's
infirmities, tempers, and constitutions. For,
it is a very hard thing for a man to work off
these. The choleric are of quick and hasty
apprehension, and readily do resent. The
phlegmatic are more dull and slow, and do not
so readily consider, they must have leisure and
time, and what is said must be often repeated:
and you must represent what you have to say,
with all advantage. Also they that are of sanguine and melancholy constitutions do not fit
each other. That which is pleasing to one is
grievous to the other. The pleasantness of the
one is not suitable to the seriousness of the
other. The melancholy temper must have time
and leisure; the sanguine temper doth all pres-

ently. Therefore we must bear with one another in those things wherein we differ, if no moral evil be there. Take every man at the best, and you will find him good for some purposes. Therefore bear with him wherein he is weak. 'Tis unmanly to take any one at a disadvantage, and very unchristian to take any man at the worst. There are incident offenses. Sometimes things fall out so crossly that one could not have imagined. Tho the thing might be well intended, yet it may happen for the worse. There are ordinary mistakes; sometimes of the things (in taking one thing or another), sometimes of the agent's part, and sometimes of the patient's side. We ourselves are often mistaken; and we acknowledge it, and say we would not have done this or that, if we had once thought, or imagined, as things are fallen out. Therefore, we must give allowance, when men mistake. There are sudden apprehensions, which should be allowed for. Some are too quick, and conceit before they have duly weighed and considered; and 'tis a hard matter to rectify a misconceit. Job's friends failed at first. They were rash in their first apprehensions, and therefore they ran on, in their severity, censure, and harsh dealings, till God interposed. Therefore take heed of the first stumble, for 'tis ominous: or, at best, a good step is lost.

He is a person very ingenious that, upon shewing, will vary from his first thoughts; for if once men have taken up an ill opinion, 'tis hard to satisfy them: by reason of which, many men run on in an error and pursue their first fault.

These are considerations that I offer for fair and equal consideration one of another, for mutual patience and fair allowance. And these things never were but in this fixt frame and temper of spirit, recommended in the text.

But now on the other hand: there are some persons that are always murmuring, complaining, and finding fault; never pleased themselves, nor pleasing others; that either are provoking or provoked; both which are to be condemned. I will not provoke, because I will leave nobody less himself than I found him; he shall not be so much the worse for my company and acquaintance. I will not be provoked, because I will not disorder myself, nor lose the composure of my own mind; than which nothing without me can be more valuable.

There seems to be an enmity to peace and quietness in some dispositions. These are malicious and turbulent spirits, whose pleasure is to make disturbance; who were never taken with the beauty of order, nor ever tasted the sweet of peace, nor framed themselves to duty

and obedience. What should such do in
heaven, where all is order and harmony?
They are only fit for the infernal hurry; company for fiends and devils, whom they exactly
resemble. In hell is darkness, perplexity, confusion. They lead a hellish life who always
are quarreling, contradicting, traducing. Yet,
some applaud themselves in this; and can they
delight in the presence of a good and merciful
God, of a compassionate Savior in the harmony of a heavenly choir, who have not been
acquainted with charity, nor exercised in love
and good will? No. They will not relish
such company nor endure their employment.
They must first be discharged of their malignity, altered in temper, reconciled to righteousness, naturalized to things of the heavenly
state, before that place can make them happy.
For place, condition, and employment, unsuit-
able to disposition, are burdensome, and can
not afford content or satisfaction; since to
heart's ease and settlement all things must
be proportionable and accommodate. They
flatter themselves greatly, they grossly cheat
and abuse themselves, who think of admittance
into God's blissful presence hereafter, or into
the society of blessed angels and glorified souls,
whose minds are not in this preparatory state,
discharged of selfishness and partiality, which
make men importune, troublesome, and very

unpleasing company. For, the pleasures of eternity are mental and intellectual, delightsome, and satisfactory, without molestation or contest.

Man is, in a sort, *felo de se*, by harboring displeasure in his breast. He makes himself uneasy by evil surmizes and discontents. If one designed to do a man the greatest mischief imaginable, one would contrive to raise in him jealousy and suspicion; to beget in him malice, ill-will, displeasure; provoke him to envy, and to malign others; he will, then, lead the life of a fiend of darkness. The malignity of his own breast will more corrode him than the sharpest humors that can infest the body.

It lies upon every one to study himself, to rectify his own temper, and where, by constitution, we are inclined to that which reason or religion can not approve, there care is to be taken to amend such inclination, and to govern it by rules of virtue: as one replied, when a physiognomer reported him vicious in several instances: "Thus (said he) I am, by bodily constitution; but, by the power of my mind, these things are subject to my reason." 'T were a reproach to a man, if a physiognomer, by viewing his countenance, or an astrologer, by casting his nativity, should tell what he is, in respect of the principles of his mind; or what he will do, upon a moral account. If so, what effect is there of principles of reason? of grounds of religion and conscience? of measures of virtue, and rules of prudence? If by study, exercise, and good use of himself, man be not better than when he came at first into the world; if there be neither improvement nor refinement; what effect is there of Christianity?

Now, I do purposely challenge, as enemies to Christianity, peevishness, frowardness, malcontentedness, which are the more dangerous evils because men warrant themselves in them; supposing there is cause for their discontent, and that they are justifiable in it. So Jonah (4:9): "I do well to be angry." This is the case of ungoverned minds and choleric constitutions.

Those who transgress in their rage and fury, when they return to themselves and to the use of sober reason, either find cause to be ashamed and to wish they had kept in better compass (which is the recovery of good nature, or virtue), or else lose themselves upon this occasion, and become more immodest and unreasonable, and more settled and confirmed in naughtiness. For good nature and the effects of it, in man, are the soil wherein the seeds of virtue being sown will grow and thrive. But let a man degenerate into hardheartedness or cruelty; virtue becomes a

Benjamin Whichcote

stranger to such a constitution. We have woful examples what monsters of rational agents on a moral account some men become, by unnatural use of themselves; wrought quite off from all ingenuity, candor, sweetness; like themselves, what they were formerly known to be. There are indeed many ways of miscarrying, for there are sails of vices; but if a man would at once spoil his nature, raze his very foundation, and absolutely indispose himself to all acts of virtue, let him allow himself in frowardness, peevishness, malcontent; let him conceive displeasure in his breast; let him bear ill-will, live in envy, malice, and out of charity (1 John 4: 8); for, since God is love, this temper is most abhorrent to him. So as that he only can dwell in God, who dwells in love (verse 16).

By discomposure of mind a person is unfit to attend upon God and incapable of enjoying him. The mind that doth contemplate God must be God-like. 'Tis only the quiet and serene mind that can contemplate God, and enjoy him; for God will not dwell where violence and fury is. We read that God was not in the fire, nor in the whirlwind, nor in the earthquake, but in the still voice (1 Kings 19: 11). And, as we are not fit to attend upon God nor to enjoy him, so likewise, not to enjoy ourselves. In such a temper, we have not the free use of our reason, nor any true content. For what is all the world to a troubled and discomposed mind? Therefore give me serenity of mind, calmness of thought; for these are better enjoyments than any thing without us. Therefore for these things will I daily praise God; for upholding the foundation of reason and understanding, which are so much in danger by the distemper of the mind; for continuing me in the privilege of liberty and freedom (for hereby I can present God with a free-will-offering, and bring unto him the consent of my mind); and for giving me power of self-enjoyment, and of taking content in myself. One may have much in the world as to right and title, and yet have nothing as to power of self-enjoyment. For in the case of misgovernment by lust, passion, and self-will, we dispossess ourselves of ourselves, and all that we may call ours.

'Tis a sinful temper, to be hard to please and ready to take offense. It is grievous to those about us, and we shall soon suffer for it; for men will soon withdraw from unquiet and turbulent spirits. Solomon hath observed, that he that would have a friend must behave himself friendly (Prov. 18:24). But these men are unacceptable everywhere; especially to those that are under them (for, as for equals, and superiors, they will soon with-draw) ; but every good man will take care of those that are under him. And upon this head I shall observe three or four things.

First, that we ought to make the lives of all those that live with us as happy and comfortable as we can, and their burdens as easy as may be. Let our advantages be never so much above theirs, and our power over them never so great, yet we should equally consider things, and do as we would be done unto, if in their circumstances.

Consider also that things may as well be done with gentleness and by fair means as otherwise ; and that things that are so done are done with pleasure and satisfaction, and will better hold ; for, things that are done by force, and with offense, will no longer last than that force continues.

There is more care to please when men are not captious, peevish, froward, or easy to take offense. Men that are often angry, and for every trifle, in a little time will be little regarded, and so lose the advantage of giving grave reproof. They will say, 'tis the manner of the person ; and, no one can help it : and so these persons will be less considered when they reprove with reason. Displeasure (when there is weighty reason for it) may prove to the offender a principle of reformation and amendment; but hasty and passionate men are not considered. Their fury is looked upon as a clap of thunder, and no one will much regard it.

Take notice what care God hath taken for the welfare and happiness of those that are inferiors, and under the power of others. The parent must not provoke his children to wrath (Eph. 6:4). Parents that have all authority over their children, must take care how they use it. The husband must not be bitter against his wife. He must give her no harsh language, but give honor to her as the weaker vessel (1 Pet. 3:7). Masters must render to their servants that which is just and equal, forbearing threatenings; knowing that they have a Master in heaven (Eph. 6:9). Then for those that labor for us, that are but for a day and are gone again, God hath required that their wages be paid them; otherwise their cry will come up into the ears of the Lord of Sabbaoth (James 5:4). Then for strangers, that are without friends, relations, or acquaintance, what care doth God take for them! Be not forgetful to entertain strangers (Heb. 13:2). Then for the widow, and the fatherless persons, that are most helpless—what care hath God taken for them? So great, that he will be revenged on those that wrong them (Ex. 22:22, 23, 24); and, on the con-

trary, will reckon those to have pure religion
and undefiled that shall visit the widows and
fatherless in their affliction (James 1:27).

This is the rule: The lower any one's condition is in the world, by so much the more he
is pitiable; and so much the greater care
should we take to ease him; he having burden
enough upon him, without any other addition
to his misery.

I will conclude this discourse with three
rules. Whosoever will do his work, with fair
words; I would not have him chid into it. I
would never blame any one for common inci-
dencies, such as might befall myself or any
one else; nor ever blame any one for not doing
that wherein he hath not particular direction.
You will say, these are low things to be spoken
in a pulpit. But let them be as low as they
will, the disorder of our minds, many times,
is occasioned for want of them; and great
disquietness is occasioned in many families
for want of that peaceable temper, which my
text speaks of.

A Prayer

Almighty God, the Father of our Lord Jesus Christ, the God of the spirits of all flesh, we profess all dependence upon thee, we live in all expectation from thee. Awaken (we entreat thee) all the powers and faculties of our souls to acts of lively sense and apprehension of thee. Call us to due diligence and careful attendance upon thee, that we may have our God highly in regard; that we may have great reverence of Deity in our minds; that we may be in the fear and apprehensions of thee while we are before thee.

1. Put us (we humbly pray thee) upon all those acts toward thee that ever thou madest us capable of, in the moment of thy creation of us; that we may duly acknowledge thee, who art the Original of our beings; that we may greatly reverence thee, who art the Father of our spirits; that we may obey thee fully, who art our Governor; that we may serve thee freely, who art our Lord and Owner; that we may be thankful unto thee, who art our great Benefactor; that we may admire and adore thee, who art a Being of all perfection; that we may love and delight in thee, who art the first and chiefest Good;

that we may place all affiance, trust, and confidence in thee, because of thy gracious promises; that we may come unto thee, in answer to thy invitation and call; that we may believe thee, who art most certain and infallible; that we may commit the great trust of our souls unto thee, because of thy known faithfulness to us; that we may rest in thee, the Center of immortal spirits; and ultimately refer to thee, who art the end of all things; and in the use of our liberty, that we may present thy majesty with a free-will offering and bring unto thee the consent of our minds; that so we may become altogether thine; that as we are thine by thy creation of us, by thy maintenance, and preservation, by thy constant providence over us, by thy gracious assuming of us into a relation to thyself by thy Son, making us the adoption of thy grace; so we may be also thine by our voluntary dedicating and devoting ourselves to thy fear and service.

2. To this purpose destroy out of us whatever we have acquired unnatural to the principles of thy creation of us, by abuse of ourselves, by neglect of thy grace, by compliance with the corrupt guise of this sinful, degenerate, and apostate world. O naturalize us to heaven, reconcile us to all the things of that high estate: that so we may not drudge in

the world, nor act in a slavish spirit in ways of religion; but that we may serve thee with ingenuity of mind, with freedom of spirit, as those that are set at liberty and delivered from the bondage and slavery of iniquity, having the law of the Spirit of life which is in Christ Jesus, making us free from the law of sin and death.

3. Blessed God, we have cause thankfully to acknowledge the divine goodness, for thou hast loved our souls from the pit of destruction; thou hast laid help for us upon one that is mighty, and every ways able to save; and hast declared thy salvation (God in Christ reconciling the world unto himself, not imputing trespasses); thou hast raised up for us a prince and a Savior, to give repentance to us, and forgiveness of sins. Now it is the language of our souls in the ears of our God; make us partakers of that salvation which thou hast appointed and which our Savior has wrought, and our souls shall bless thee to eternity.

4. To this purpose bring us within the terms of the covenant of grace (repentance from dead works, resolved obedience in all things to God, and faith in the Lord Jesus Christ) and suffer us not herein to fail or to fall short. Give us heartily and sincerely to revoke and undo whatsoever we have done

amiss in life; to condemn ourselves for doing those things, to deprecate thy just offense and displeasure; to cry thee mercy; to ask thee pardon; and for all time to come, to leave off to sin, and to return to our duty.

5. And let us herein be gainers by our former losses and miscarriages, to make us more sensible of our weakness and inability, and of our necessary dependence upon thee our God: to be more thankful unto thee for thy gracious interposure, in preventing of us from running into those evils that we have not committed; to be modest and humble in the sense of our former miscarriages; to be cautious and wary, that in time to come we do not transgress; and to make us more charitable and compassionate to our brethren, that in many things may have failed as well as we.

6. Give us carefully to hold the Head of the Church, and to make all due acknowledgments to the Savior of the body mystical; help us to conceive of him, for the height and excellency of his person, for the worthiness and fulness of his undertaking and performance on our behalf, according as we ought. Let us have that dependence upon him, that expectation by him, that thou hast warranted us to have; and make that use of him, that thou hast set him up for; both that our faith and hope may finally rest in God, as also that

we may be planted into the likeness of his death, by mortification, self-denial, self-surrender; and may bear the image of his resurrection, by spirituality and heavenly mindedness; that so he may become a complete Savior to us, we having redemption through his blood, the forgiveness of sins, and the renovation of our natures by the operation of his good spirit.

7. Bring us, we humbly pray thee, to the truth of a creature-state, humility, and modesty: clothe our minds with that humility that befits creatures, with that modesty that becomes sinners. Suffer us not to be vainly fraught nor possest; to be giddily minded, or intoxicated with fond conceits. O let us not live in a lie, flatter ourselves, deceiving our own souls, promising that of ourselves, or of any other creature, that will not prove true.

Help us all along in life to subordinate all the affairs and transactions of time to serve the interest of our souls in the state that is before us. Help us to shake off this vain world, and to breathe after eternity, immortality, and glory; being in perfect reconciliation with the law of everlasting righteousness, goodness, and truth, which are the laws of heaven; so shall we comply with thy nature, mind, and will, and fully answer the relation we stand in to thee. Relieve and ease our consciences by the blood of sprinkling, according to our several conditions of body and mind; supply us with suitable grace and strength.

8. We are, O Lord, thy care and charge; thou undertakest for us; we confess and acknowledge that we are in nothing self-sufficient; not wise enough for our own direction, not able enough for our own defense, nor yet good enough for our own satisfaction. We came into being at thy call, we continue in being at thy maintenance and allowance, and we shall go out of these beings which now we have, at thine appointment; and it will not be in our power to withhold our souls from thee one moment, tho the state and welfare of them to all eternity did depend thereupon.

9. Help us therefore to acknowledge thee in all our ways, and not to lean to our own understandings. Teach us, blessed God, so to number our days, as to apply our hearts unto wisdom; and to mind those things which are in conjunction with our everlasting welfare. Take us out of an earthly and worldly spirit, and give us sense spiritually exercised, that we may favor and relish, judge and discern, the ways and things of God. O, let us be always under thy communication and influence; so in the light of thy countenance at-

tract and draw us to thyself; and stay us with thee, and suffer us never to depart from thee, upon any temptation, provocation, or suggestion whatsoever.

O Lord, communicate thy light to our minds, thy life to our souls; as thou art original to us by thy creation of us, so be thou also final by our intention of thee.

10. Go over the workmanship of thy creation in us again; to mend all the defects we have contracted, and to destroy out of us by the working of thy grace and spirit whatsoever we have acquired unnatural to thy creation of us. Transform us into the image of thy Son, conform us to his likeness, make us, body and soul, an habitation for thyself, by thy Holy Spirit.

Make thy Son to us all which thou hast appointed him to be unto sinners. Make him to us wisdom, that we who have played the fool, by consenting to iniquity, and giving our good God an offense, may better understand ourselves in the great concernments of our souls. Make him to us righteousness, that we may be out of danger, by reason of the deserved punishment of our sin. Make him to us sanctification, that we who have marred our spirits and spoiled our principles, by unnatural use, may inwardly be made whole and renewed in the spirit of our minds. Make him to us redemption, that we may be set at liberty, and delivered from the tyranny of sin and Satan, who hath many times led us captive.

11. We thank thee for the happy terms of the covenant of grace; terms that are good in themselves and fit for thy creatures, such as our own hearts can not desire better or other. For what is it that the Lord our God doth require of us, but only those things which are necessary to our everlasting welfare? Neither hast thou denied us any thing but what is for our hurt and prejudice. O, bring us into thy good terms, and suffer us not herein to fail, or fall short.

12. We bless thee for that good hand which thou hast held over us by day and by night, at home and abroad, alone and in company; that thou hast put away evil things from us, and conferred many good things upon us in great kindness, tenderness, and compassion. For either the evil things that threatened us have not come at all; or if they have come, they have not continued so long as we suspected nor have been so great as we imagined; or else thou hast over-ruled them, subdued, and turned them unto good; and for good things, thou hast even transcended our hopes, and exceeded our expectations. O, be thou endeared and recommended to us by thy good-

ness, kindness, and faithfulness; and let us be engaged unto thee in duty and affection, that so with choice and delight we may live to that God by whom we live.

13. We thank thee that we have the use of our reason and understanding in which many fail, that we have power of self-enjoyment, and taking content in our lives; that thou hast given us power to choose and determine ourselves; and that thou hast permitted our choice.

We acknowledge, that if in any thing our conditions are better or easier than the conditions of those that are most miserable and necessitous, that herein the goodness of the Lord our God hath been extended toward us; for we have used ourselves as venturously, and run as many hazards, as others; and but for thy gracious interposure, we might have been as miserable as others.

14. Acquaint us, blessed God, in this day of our exercise, probation, and trial, with the employment of eternity (conversation with our God by holy meditation, by heavenly ejaculations, by constant intention of God, his honor and service; by exact walking according to the difference of good and evil; and by frequent application to thee by prayer, and all other holy exercises), that so when these frail bodies of ours shall fall away and

tumble into the dust and leave our souls alone, and when there shall be no more either of bodily employment or concernment, that our souls may then readily adjoin themselves unto these immediate attendants upon God, the angels, and saints in glory ; and in that blessed comfort spend eternity in singing praises and hallelujahs to that God, of whose grace and goodness we have had so great experience all along in life.

15. Help us so to order our conversation in the world, so to govern our spirits, and to lead such lives, upon which we may safely die; and when we shall come to leave the world, afford us such a mighty power and presence of thy own good Spirit, that we may have solid consolation in believing, and depart in the faith of God's elect. That we may escape the dreadful pangs of death, all consternation of mind, all confusion of thoughts, all doubtfulness and uncertainty concerning our everlasting condition; that so we may cheerfully follow thee into the estate on the other side of death, of which thou hast given us so great assurance by the resurrection of our Lord and Savior Jesus Christ, who hath brought life and immortality to light by the gospel, and who hath promised to change these our vile bodies, that they may be fashioned like unto his glorious body, accord-

ing to the working of his mighty power, by which he is able to subdue all things unto himself; and, Lord, give us in the meantime in faith and patience to possess our souls.

16. We are daily admonished, as by years growing upon some of us, so by experience and observation abroad every day, one or other taken away from our society, converse, and acquaintance; and sometimes persons of fewer years, and of greater strength, and more likely to live than ourselves; neither do we know how it comes to pass that we survive them, nor how long it will be, ere we shall follow them, nor yet what matter of disease may be gathering together in these base and vile bodies of ours, which tho we feel them not to-day, may appear to-morrow. Lord, keep us in consideration hereof, and the reference of time to eternity, to apply our hearts unto wisdom; and to mind those things that are in conjunction with our everlasting welfare.

17. And superadd this to all the grace and favor thou hast shown us all along in life, not to remove us hence but with all advantages for eternity, when we shall be in due preparation of mind, in a holy disposition of soul, in a perfect renunciation of the guise of this mad and sinful world; when we shall be entirely resigned up unto thee our God; when we shall have clear acts of faith in God

by Jesus Christ in our souls, high and reverential thoughts of thee in our minds, enlarged and inflamed affections toward thee.

18. Wherefore, blessed God, consummate the work of thy grace which thou hast begun in our souls; perfect the cure thou hast begun upon our minds; and then when thou shalt have brought us to glory, we who through our earthliness, carnality, and folly, have been weary of a little attendance upon thee in time, shall think eternity itself too strait and too narrow for us to bless and magnify so good a God, so well-deserving at our hands.

19. Do good unto the whole world, recover thy lapsed creation, compassionate the forlorn condition of mankind, lost in themselves, and lost to God, through ignorance, stupidity, and senselessness, where persons have never been awakened; through superstition, idolatry, and false worship, wherein many have been nursed up, and bred; through atheism, dissoluteness and profaneness, whereby they have made havoc of conscience.

20. O let the light of the glorious gospel of Christ break forth and shine throughout the whole world: fulfil the promise thou hast made unto the Messiah, that thou wilt give him the heathen for his inheritance, and the utmost parts of the earth for his possession; that the wolf shall dwell with the lamb, and

that the leopard shall lie down with the kid, the calf and the young lion and the fatling together; that they shall not hurt nor destroy in all thy holy mountain: but that there may be a perfect dwelling together in love, harmony, and reconciliation with the whole creation.

21. Reform all things amiss in these kingdoms: control atheism, irreligion and profaneness; establish peace, truth, and righteousness; frustrate all naughty designs; suffer us not to be hurried back again to . . . superstition, or any false worship; but settle us in the purity of our religion, and our just rights.

Restrain the sons of violence, that turn all into confusion, and that make havoc and desolation in the family of God.

22. Direct him whom thou hast placed on the throne, etc.; furnish him with all divine gifts and graces that may sanctify his soul here and save him hereafter. Bless him and us in all his royal family, etc.

23. Compassionate all in misery and affliction, especially such whose cases we are acquainted with; comfort, help, and restore, O Lord, be thou a present help to them in any needful time of trouble: such as lie upon sick beds, direct those that are about them to proper and fit means for their recovery, and add thy blessing; take not them nor us out of

this state till thou hast fitted and qualified us for the state of immortality, eternity, and glory.

24. Assist us now in the service we are met to perform, that we, beginning in the name and fear of God, may be promoted by divine assistance, encouraged by thy acceptance, and end in thy glory and the advantage of our immortal souls.

Grant that which shall be now spoken according to thy will may be received as from thyself, and turned to the information of our understandings, wherein any of us have been mistaken; the refining of our spirits, the right ordering of the actions of our lives and conversations; that God in all things may be glorified, and our souls finally saved in the day of our Lord Jesus Christ, by whom we are bold to call thee Father, etc.

A Prayer of Gottfried Arnold

O most merciful God and Father, we commend ourselves and all that we have to thine almighty hands, and pray thee to preserve us by thy good Spirit from all sin, misfortune, and grief of heart. Give us the spirit of grace and prayer, that we may have a consoling trust in thy love, and that our sighs and petitions may be acceptable in thy sight. Give us the spirit of faith to kindle a bright flame of true and blessed faith in our hearts, that we may have a living knowledge of salvation, and our whole life may be a thank-offering for the mercies we have received. Give us the spirit of love, that we may experience the sweetness of thy love toward us, and also love thee in return, and render our obedience not from constraint like slaves, but with the willing and joyful hearts of children. AMEN.